PREFACE

The original drafts of this book were written before the writing of the classroom material published as **'Towards Mathematics'**. The reason for working in this way was to enable the authors to prepare jointly a basic philosophy for the teaching of mathematics in the Primary School. This philosophy was then turned into a practical form in the writing of the various components of the packs. During the six years taken in compiling **'Towards Mathematics'** and testing it with children, the original philosophy was expanded and developed, and this book has been rewritten to incorporate these extended ideas.

Both authors contributed to all the material of the project and revised each other's work to the extent that it would be difficult in retrospect to say who wrote what. When the stage of publication was reached, however, it was necessary for a single hand to be responsible for the final text. David Sturgess undertook the task of editing the classroom material and associated Handbooks, rearranging and rewriting to make a coherent whole. John Glenn has similarly taken responsibility for the final form of this book.

John Glenn
David Sturgess

A Primary Teacher's Guide

TOWARDS
MATHEMATICS

J. A. Glenn

and

D. A. Sturgess

 Schofield & Sims Ltd

First printed 1977

0041993

112516

374·51
GLE

Designed and produced in England by Peter Sinclair (Design and Print) Ltd

CONTENTS

INTRODUCTION

The introduction of new methods and topics into the mathematics of the Primary School has given rise to two main criticisms. One is that pupils begin secondary work without the number skills that are essential for progress, the other is that topics are introduced in order to swell a syllabus without ever forming part of a coherent scheme of mathematical knowledge.

Any proposed scheme of mathematics must try to meet these two criticisms.

Elementary mathematics once meant only arithmetic, a complete set of rules developed for doing addition, subtraction, multiplication and other processes. These have been passed on from teacher to pupil over generations. In most cases there are no stated mathematical reasons for these rules; they are only algorithms for enabling one to get correct answers. This is no longer sufficient in an age when the prime requirement is for people who can think originally and tackle new problems confidently.

Recent years have seen a welcome attempt to improve on this situation. It is true, nevertheless, that the development of new approaches to mathematics at primary level was marked at first by considerable disagreement about both content and method. Some topics, like set theory, were either given detailed treatment or rejected completely as useless and abstract; some methods found themselves dismissed as mere rote learning and others criticized as haphazard and incompetent. Behind much of the discussion was an uncertainty about the aim of primary mathematics teaching, whether it should restrict itself to a thorough training in computational skills as a foundation on which the subject could be developed at secondary levels, or whether it should attempt to develop an understanding of principles that could allow skills as such to develop in their own time.

The new syllabuses and methods have now been in use long enough to be capable of assessment, and one can see a broad agreement about content, about what in the older courses can be omitted or relaxed and which of the new topics can be selected for inclusion. There is less agreement about method and aim, and one still finds the new topics taught using traditional methods of instruction.

The existence of a class textbook tends to impose a method of teaching based on it, yet without textbooks it is difficult to achieve a systematic and coherent course.

This book has a double purpose. It discusses for the benefit of teachers a course which includes a whole range of mathematical activities suitable for primary school children, and it provides the background philosophy for the material of **'Towards Mathematics'** by developing the ideas at a length which is not possible in the teacher's handbook to the children's text.

The book is independent of the children's texts and will, it is hoped, be useful to anyone planning a scheme of work at primary level, whether for an individual class or the whole school. Those teachers who choose to use **'Towards Mathematics'** will find in this book additional material to aid them in the discussions with children and in guiding them through the texts. The structure of **'Towards Mathematics'** is discussed briefly in an appendix.

The view taken throughout this book and the associated texts is that mathematics is a cumulative and not a linear study. There is no sequencing of ideas and activities which is desirable for all children on either mathematical or pedagogical grounds. A particular mathematical idea often depends on many others. For example, in order to use the concept of area, a child needs to have available concepts of measurement, length and multiplication of number, but it does not matter in what order these other concepts have been acquired. What is important is that these other concepts should be secure before area is studied. This non-linear view of mathematics means that there is a wide and genuine choice of activities for young children and teachers at all stages of learning. In this book and the associated texts of **'Towards Mathematics'** the material is developed so that a large number of activities are available in parallel, and that both teachers and children have a choice of activity in spite of the order necessarily imposed by putting together a book.

Chapter 1

LEARNING MATHEMATICS

1 The nature of mathematical activity

The ways in which children learn are complex and certainly not fully understood, but new insights into the learning process are always being discovered.
As a result of the work of many researchers in education, we now have a picture
which enables us to discuss the nature of mathematical activity and the ways in
which it is learnt by children.

The work of Jean Piaget on children's concept formation has shown that
many of the ideas used in mathematics, which appear quite obvious to us as
adults, are not in fact obvious at all to children. Simple ideas such as mass and
volume are not suddenly grasped by the child, but are formed over a number of
years by abstracting the concepts from a wide variety of experiences. More
complex ideas, such as that of place value in number notation, call for long use
before they are fully understood. The knowledge that a teacher possesses of
Piaget's findings can be used to help him understand that if a child has not fully
grasped something it may not be because of laziness or stupidity, but because the
child has not formed a basic concept and is not ready to proceed with further
ideas. It is not true that if a certain range of experiences is provided the child will
automatically abstract a concept. The formation of concepts is a continuous
process and happens only when the child has reached a certain stage of understanding. The child should, however, be given as rich an environment as is
possible, and will then have a much greater opportunity for abstracting concepts. Also, by working as far as possible with individuals, it will be far easier for
the teacher to be aware of the different stages of development of the children,
and to cater for these differences.

There are two recognisable threads running through the learning of mathematics from the Infant School to the University. These are the learning of established mathematical ideas and the mathematics which the child or the student is
creating. The two threads depend heavily on one another, although at various
stages of the learning process one will be more important than the other for a
short space of time. For the infant and young junior the creation of mathematics
by the children themselves is very important. There comes a stage, which varies
from child to child, when he wishes to have computational skills (such as long
multiplication) at his disposal in order to be able to solve problems, and it is
then that these techniques are most efficiently learnt.

This may seem to some teachers to be a haphazard procedure (which it is) and
a risky one (which it is not). For the majority of the children leaving the Primary
School the most important asset they can have is experience of all kinds of
mathematical activity and confidence in applying mathematical methods to the

solution of problems. If this experience is sound and the child is really confident then techniques and knowledge of mathematical ideas can be acquired quickly and efficiently at the secondary stage. This is not to say that children at the later stages do not need to create their own mathematics.

In order to understand what is meant by 'the child creating his own mathematics', it is necessary to consider the whole nature of mathematical activity. For many people mathematics is 'sums' and nothing more. They believe that all that needs to be done to improve mathematics teaching is to devise better ways of doing sums. Many Primary teachers have been discovering over the last few years that there is far more than this to mathematics, but it is still difficult to pin down exactly what has replaced the 'sums'.

Consider an example. One of the activities frequently suggested in texts is that of putting coloured plastic pegs in the holes of a piece of peg board, and it is important to ask what aspects of this activity can be described as 'mathematical'. In order to answer this question completely one would need to know exactly why a child performs the actions that he does, and this is usually not possible because either the child himself does not know, or he is unable to explain his reasons. If, however, one watches the children and discusses with them what they are doing, several things emerge. Putting the pegs into the board in a completely random way is probably no more than just discovering what patterns are made when the pegs are put in the board. The child will next start to make patterns either using the colours of the pegs or the position of the pegs on the board, or a mixture of both. If the pattern-making is conscious (i.e. the pegs are put into a particular place in order to make a particular pattern, rather than the pattern emerging as the pegs are put in in a random way), then this could be a recall of a previous experience with shapes. The child may be constructing 'stars' or 'crosses' with the pegs.

This kind of activity is very necessary since the child is creating his own patterns and has a choice of how he makes these patterns, but it may not have any great mathematical significance. If, however, the child starts asking questions about the activity, or tries to classify various shapes, then this becomes a *mathematical* activity of a much more general nature. For instance, if he discovers that with three pegs he can either put them in a straight line or at the vertices of a triangle, he has discovered something which is an important geometrical property when, at a later stage, the geometry of points and lines is being considered.

In this kind of situation the child is best left to pursue his own lines of exploration rather than to have the situation structured to lead to some predetermined end point. In free exploration of this kind it is not always possible to determine what the children have discovered from any particular activity and, in some cases, it provides an experience which will only become important in the light of later experiences. It is certainly not true that all such experiences are mathematically or educationally important and the following are suggested as guide lines to help the teacher to place a value, albeit a subjective one, on the children's exploration and discovery.

There are certain conceptual ideas that are quite general, in that they appear in many disciplines, but in which mathematics is especially rich. A complete list would be a long one, but the following are some of the more important.

1 Classification
2 Generalisation
3 Symbolisation
4 Transformation

Other activities of a different kind are:

5 Hypothesis making and testing
6 Proof

1 Classification

When a group of problems or objects such as shapes are identified as having a 'sameness' then one can put them together and give them a name. One classifies certain shapes as being 'rectangular', certain problems as being 'addition problems'. Classification is a basic mathematical activity and children from an early age need to be given the experience of deciding what is the 'same' and what is 'different' about all kinds of entities. It is not sufficient merely to learn the names that have already been given, such as 'odds', 'evens', 'isosceles triangles', but to explore sameness and difference in all areas as an activity in its own right.

2 Generalisation

There are numerous patterns in mathematics and in particular in the various number systems, e.g. the products of 9 are 9, 18, 27, 36, 45 ... If one adds the digits of each product these come to 9. Is this always true? Will it be true for 154×9 say? If one can find a general pattern of this nature, then one can write a general statement of the fact.

To take another example

$$1+2+3=6$$
$$1+2+3+4=10$$
$$1+2+3+4+5=15 \text{ and so on.}$$

What is $1+2+3+4+\ldots+n$?

There are various ways of showing that the last sum is $\frac{n}{2}(n+1)$ and *this* is the generalisation.

This last is a formal statement of a generalisation which is only suitable for the older and brighter children in a primary school, if at all, but the *activity* of looking for generalisations is one that can take place at all levels of ability and at all ages.

3 Symbolisation

Mathematics is unique in the extent to which it uses symbols as the actual material on which abstract operations are performed. If one has 5 apples and adds 6 more apples one finds the total by adding 5 and 6, $5+6=11$. We do this whether the original objects are apples, pears, bananas or monkeys. The statement $5+6=11$ is quite independent of the objects from which it arose. Most of the symbols that children meet are already decided by common usage and it would be inconvenient to use, say, ∗ for addition. There are, however, situations in which the children work with concepts for which there is no accepted symbol,

13

and in these cases they should be encouraged to invent suitable ones. In every case children should be encouraged to practise the expression of problems in a symbolic form, from the simple '5 apples add 6 apples' to more complex problems involving several operations. This again is a key mathematical activity.

4 Transformation

Many mathematical processes depend upon transforming a problem into an equivalent problem that may have an easier or more direct solution, e.g.

  i $34-27$ is equivalent to $(20+14)-(20+7)$ which is equivalent to $14-7$

  ii $3+5=8$ is equivalent to $8-5=3$
  or $8-3=5$

  iii $24\div7=x$ is equivalent to $7\times x=24$

  iv $\frac{1}{2}+\frac{1}{4}$ is equivalent to $\frac{2}{4}+\frac{1}{4}$

  v The area of a triangle is equivalent to that of a rectangle. This is shown for a particular case by the following diagram.

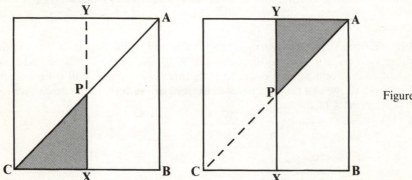

Figure 1.1

The shaded part PXC of the triangle ABC is cut off and fitted into the space APY so that the triangle is transformed into the rectangle ABXY.

There is, of course, no subject or topic named 'Transformation' that needs to be taught. It is another basic activity that appears in many guises and should be one of the tools that children use naturally.

When a child is involved in some form of investigation or discovery, questions that a teacher can ask himself to help him to put a value on that activity are 'is he classifying?'; 'is he generalising?' or 'symbolising?' or 'transforming?' If the child is doing any of these things, then it is extremely likely that the activity will be mathematically valuable.

5 Hypothesis making and testing

When faced, say, with a number property which one wants to generalise, then one must ask the question whether it is *always* true. If one answers this question rigorously, then one has provided a proof; but formal proof is not suitable for all but a tiny minority of primary school children. It is, however, possible to sow the seeds for the formal proofs that will come later by a sensible process of hypothesis making and testing. A hypothesis is 'an informed guess'; something that it is reasonable to assume on the basis of what is known, but which has to be tested for confirmation.

For example, if one marks on a 100 square the numbers which are multiples of 2 (the set M_2, say), and also those which are multiples of 3 (the set M_3), then one finds by trial that the numbers which are common to both sets are also multiples of 6. That is, they are members of the set M_6. It is now a reasonable hypothesis that numbers common to the two sets M_2 and M_4 belong to the set M_8, i.e. that multiples of both 2 and 4 are multiples of 8. If this hypothesis is tested it proves to be wrong.

One can now try further sets of multiples and try to form a hypothesis that does stand up to testing. Note that one can disprove a hypothesis by showing a single contrary instance, but that the accumulation of successful tests does not constitute a *proof*, only a confirmation.

6 Proof

Not many means of proof are available to young children, but one very useful one is appeal to the concrete situation from which a number pattern, say, has arisen. For example, if one makes a square pattern of 8 pegs on a pegboard and then makes another square to surround it, double the number of pegs are used. Will this always be so? Examine the figure.

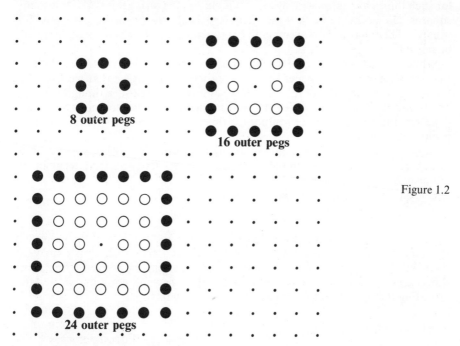

Figure 1.2

Trial shows that doubling is the wrong hypothesis. A new hypothesis would be that 8 pegs are added each time. This can be checked by making the next square and it appears correct. But will it always be true? A satisfactory form of proof

15

can be provided by looking at the actual physical situation and seeing how a new square can be formed from the previous one.

If the pegs of one square are moved outward to form a new square so that the pegs on each side are *moved in exactly the same way* one gets this

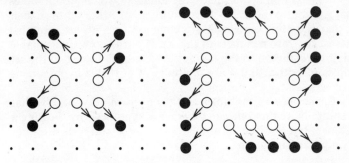

Figure 1.3

We can now see that in each case there will be 8 holes that need to be filled to complete the next square. This physical pattern gives a justification for the hypothesis which provides a form of proof.

Another method of proof available is proof by exhaustion which means we test the hypothesis with *every possible situation*. This method is usually not applicable to number patterns since the possibilities are infinite, but is possible for such things as shapes with a small number of pins on a geoboard. How many squares can be made on a 9-pin geoboard is shown by making all possible squares. There has to be a systematic approach to this, however, or squares will be missed.

When proof is not possible, then it must be made quite clear to the children that the strength of our belief in the hypothesis can only be that we have not found a case to contradict it, and that such a case can exist, although we have not found it. Since much scientific and mathematical development has taken place resulting from just such a situation, this would seem a perfectly satisfactory position to hold.

Great care must be taken in not assuming the truth of hypotheses on too little evidence. One kind of example often given is to find the next term in an unfinished series.

Consider for example, the series beginning

> 3   6   12   24   48 . . .

Most readers would suggest 96 as the next term and this is so if the pattern in the mind of whoever wrote it was 'begin with 3 and double each term to arrive at the next'. It *could*, however, be a more complicated pattern arrived at by taking differences between successive terms until they become constant at 3. After repeating the operation four times one would then have

3	6	12	24	48	93	171	
	3	6	12	24	45	78	First differences
		3	6	12	21	33	Second differences
			3	6	9	12	Third differences
				3	3	3	Fourth differences

The next terms in this pattern are 93 and 171 instead of 96 and 192. The example may seem complicated, but it does show clearly that there is no one hypothesis about the way the series should continue. Sometimes the series could arise from a *physical* situation which bypasses the need for a hypothesis – for example, a colony of bacteria which doubles its numbers at a given rate – but without the prior situation there is no check.

An area in which it is important to ensure that some mathematical activity takes place is that of practical measurement such as weighing. It is quite possible for children to be happily engaged in practical activities which have little or no mathematical value, as such. For example, using a measuring tape to measure the classroom is only an exercise in the technique of measurement if no questions are asked other than 'how long?' or 'how wide is the classroom?' This, of course, is a necessary activity and needs to be done, but it is not 'mathematical'. It becomes a mathematical activity if the formation of some concept of the particular lengths is involved, or it leads to some work on scale drawing, or, most important of all, it takes place because the information gathered is necessary for the solution of a problem. A well-known and interesting activity for older children is the placing of masses in a scale pan attached to a spring or to an elastic band and measuring the stretch of the band for different values. This, by itself, is not a mathematical activity, but it becomes one if we ask questions such as "does the same thing happen for all springs or all bands?" This question is still a physical one, but when it is asked the child is faced with a problem. One, but not the only way of solving this problem, is to draw a graph and see if there is a relation between the mass and the stretch which will enable one to predict what the stretch will be for a given mass and to see from the patterns whether all bands and springs behave in similar ways. Note that the question poses the problem. This is quite different from the type of science 'experiment' that used to be done in schools where the pupil merely checks the stated results experimentally and avoids the problem of bringing mathematics into action..

2   The role of the teacher

The additional emphasis being placed upon the understanding of concepts, the insistence that children pursue the various activities in a way that ensures involvement in mathematical activity, implies a change in the role of the teacher. It is no longer sufficient to impart knowledge and see that the children practise the skills they have been shown; the teacher will now want to be aware of the stage of learning which each individual pupil has reached and to provide experiences which will lead him to the next stage at the right moment. Such a role requires great skill and judgement and it is difficult for any teacher to be aware of the precise stage which each child in a class has reached at a given time, let alone to provide a different type of work for each child depending on his ability and level of development. In the circumstances, the teacher has to compromise by having children working in groups rather than as individuals and by using texts, work cards and projects as a primary source for providing tasks for the children.

At one time text books, at least in arithmetic and mathematics, were used merely as sources of examples. They often contained explanations and exposition, but teachers usually preferred to give their own exposition of a process, following it with examples taken from the book and worked by the pupils.

But only the teacher can initiate *discussion*. There are some things that the written word can achieve and other things that it cannot. In developing concepts such as generalisation, classification and proof, the most important medium is the discussion between child and child and between child and teacher. To find sufficient examples to test a hypothesis can be a very frustrating individual experience, even if the child understands what is wanted. As a joint activity between a number of children, however, it can be an exciting exploration, since one child will think of possibilities that do not occur to others. The start to mathematical investigations is often very simple questions like, "How many . . .?" "What happens if . . .?" "Does it always go on?" and "What would it be for 10, 100, for n?" and this type of question when asked by the teacher as part of a conversation has a clear context and the child will understand what is required of him even if he cannot answer. A child will only answer a question in a book if it demands a direct answer. The kinds of question given above cannot, however, be asked as part of a written instruction (although they may be suitable for exceptional children), and because of the lack of discussion, a child does not know what is intended. The response to a question like those printed on a work card or in a text is nearly always, "What does this mean?"

The size of the class with which most primary school teachers work means that only a short time can be spent on discussion with any individual child.

The discussions that the teacher will want to have will probably be of several kinds:

1 To explore at a greater depth some investigation already embarked on by the child.

2 To check that work correctly done has been understood.

3 To explain in a different way work that has not been understood.

4 To suggest some project of a larger scale that uses skills acquired from the written material.

5 To keep a check on the development stages reached by individual children.

6 To initiate activities involving classification, generalisation and proof, etc.

Since the teacher will also want to keep records of the children's progress, he is faced with a daunting programme, which leaves little time for exposition and preparation of mathematical activities. This means that texts and work cards need to be used as the means of initiating such activities for the children as they become ready for them. The ideal written material is one that will take over the initial teaching role as far as content and skills are concerned and leave the teacher free to pursue the role that *only* he or she can perform, that of discussing work with the children and initiating the next step, if possible adapted to the needs of each child according to his interests and abilities.

Chapter 2

NUMBER : THE BASIC CONCEPTS

1 Classification and counting

Many children count before they begin to attend school, although only a few can write the number symbols. Since counting implies a collection of objects, usually brought together because of some attribute which happens to be relevant – for example, all the names on a list or all the counters in a box – the discussion begins with the concept of a 'set'.

In ordinary speech the word 'set' usually means a specified collection, as of an issue of stamps, which is incomplete if any item is missing, but in the technical sense it is more general.

In mathematics, a set is any collection of objects, tangible or abstract, which obeys two rules.

1 The objects must be distinguishable one from the other, if only by position like the points on a graph.

2 There must be a criterion which decides whether or not any given object belongs or does not belong to the set.

The objects which make up a set are called its *members*, or sometimes its *elements*.

There are no rules about what should make the members of a set; it could be numbers, words, people, statues, etc. One could even have abstract ideas such as 'feeling happy' but it is difficult to say in this case with any conviction what is or is not a member of the set.

Examples of sets are

1 {1, 2, 3}

2 {2, 4, 6}

3 {a, e, i, o, u}

4 {knife, fork, spoon}

5 {elephant, wrist-watch, lump of cheese}

The braces show that the objects enclosed by them are to be considered as a set: this is a standard notation.

In these examples one could give a collective name for all except the last one; 1 the first three whole numbers; 2 the first three even numbers; 3 the vowels; 4 cutlery. These are all sets purely and simply because they have been put together, and the last example makes the point that the members of a set do not have to be related although, in fact, sets which possess a certain common property are the most useful kind.

Notice that the order in which the members are named is not important: {a, e, i, o, u} is just as good as {e, o, i, a, u}. If, for any reason, the members have to be put in a given order, the set is called an *ordered set*.

Some sets have so many members that any listing or counting would be quite impossible in practice. An example would be

the set of all ants in Great Britain at the present moment.

Certain other sets, called infinite sets, cannot be counted even in principle, because one can go on adding to the set without conceivable end. Examples would be

1   the set of all whole numbers,

2   the set of multiples of two.

It is usual to label sets by capital letters, so that a convenient shorthand for some examples given earlier could be

A = {1, 2, 3}

B = {2, 4, 6}

and one could add a set

C = {1, 2, 3, 4, 5}.

Note that all the members of A are also found in C. A is then said to be a *subset* of C. Sometimes two sets match up to one another in a way that is commonly found and quite familiar. Every cup in a set of cups on a meal table rests in a saucer which belongs to the set of saucers. This relationship, where to each member of one set there corresponds one member of another, is called *one-to-one correspondence*. It is the key concept of the counting process. Many educational toys for young children, in which, for example, plugs are fitted into holes, are designed to demonstrate this.

It is important to note that one-to-one correspondence by itself does not imply counting. It can, in some situations, answer questions more easily than by counting. If, for example, in a hall full of people the chairs are in well-spaced rows, one can see at a glance whether any are not occupied or whether people are standing. One could then answer without counting the question whether there are as many people as chairs.

When an exact one-to-one correspondence can be shown between two sets, they are said to be *numerically equivalent*. The equivalence is also described by saying that the sets have the *same cardinal number*.

From here, the logical step to counting can be seen. In counting, objects are put into one-to-one correspondence with an ordered set of words called 'number words'. The cardinal number of any set is taken as the last word of the ordered set of number words. In order to count accurately, there are two distinct requirements to be met

1   the number words must be known in the correct order;

2   the objects counted must be put into one-to-one correspondence with the words.

It can now be seen why it must be possible to distinguish between the members of a set. A child has great difficulty in counting even a small collection of objects if he does not pick them up and put them aside as he counts. Adults find difficulty if the set is large and irregular, and the difficulty increases tremendously if the objects are moving about as in a playground full of children. One can also see the need for classification; it is the prior sorting out of the set of objects that are to be counted, from the set of all objects with which the child is confronted.

Nobody should think that counting is a simple process. It is easy to assume that if a child knows the number words, he can count. A child who has learnt to associate number words with sets of dots in patterns, such as the pattern $\therefore$ for 'five', or even to associate numbers only with sets of *similar* objects, such as 'six black kittens, seven green balls . . .', may well have failed to grasp the technique of putting the words into one-to-one correspondence with any set of objects.

Initially, the number symbols may be taken as merely shorthand for the words. It is quicker to write '3 men' than 'three men', '5 dogs' rather than 'five dogs'. In both, the cardinal number is associated with an actual set of objects.

Arithmetic itself differs from the verbal use of number words in two ways:

   1 it uses a special set of symbols in making number statements;
   2 it detaches the symbols from association with actual objects and studies abstract relationships between the symbols themselves.

'Two cats and three dogs' is a verbal expression involving animals; $2+3$ is an arithmetical expression involving symbols. The child learns to attach meaning to $2+3$ subconsciously by abstracting from his early experience in sorting and classifying objects into sets, and from his later experience in counting them. Arithmetic, as such, is not about material objects, but arises from the numerical properties common to all sets.

By sorting and classifying the objects of his world, by counting them and recording the count in symbols, the child builds up the background of number sense that forms the basis of arithmetic. Until he can count easily and accurately, he is not ready to do arithmetic.

A special difficulty in passing from counting operations to arithmetical processes lies in dealing with zero. In mathematical language, we say that zero is the cardinal number of the *empty set*. This merely means that, if a specified set has no members, then the *number* of its members is zero. Zero provides an answer and a corresponding recording symbol to such questions as "How many currants are there in a madeira cake?" or, "How many pupils are absent from a class if all are in attendance?"

The last example is worth discussing with children. The symbol 0, or the written word NONE, gives the so-called *null return*. It means that the question has been attended to and the answer is zero or none. Without it the question could have been forgotten or the return lost.

Another concept expressed numerically is that of ordinality. Often objects such as the words in a sentence or the notes in a tune are put in the correct order quite automatically. Many children's games impose an order on the players by putting them into correspondence with the words of a jingle, such as the familiar 'eeny, meeny, miny, mo . . .'. The number words have an inner order of succession, and hence are used as a standard sequence for ordering. This gives the *ordinal numbers*, the cardinals suitably modified,

   first, second, third, fourth, fifth . . . .

The use of the ordinals should parallel the use of the cardinals, so that the words just given should become familiar to the child soon after he becomes familiar with counting. He would probably learn *first* and *second* very early in life.

It is worth noting that in spite of their usefulness the ordinal numbers as such are not arithmetical entities, and do not obey arithmetical rules. For example, $1+2=3$ but 1st together with 2nd does not make 3rd.

Numbers also have uses which are not really mathematical at all. For example, numbers are used as labels for convenient identification as with 'part numbers' on a spares list. Here the serial order, as with registration numbers of cars, merely provides a pattern of reference, like the alphabetical arrangement in an English dictionary. Numbers can also be used as codes. The sequence of digits in a telephone number marks out a coded route through a network of connections in an automatic telephone exchange to the required subscriber. Armies and large businesses number their personnel to avoid confusion between like names. It could be a valuable exercise for older children to make a list of all the uses of number they can find, apart from its basic uses in counting and computation.

2 Notation and place value

Once it is accepted that counting a set is putting its members into one-to-one correspondence with a standard ordered set of number words, there emerges more than one possible way of constructing these numbers.

Firstly, different number words and symbols could be devised and extended as required for use without any repetitive pattern. The first twenty symbols each representing a word in a language could have been

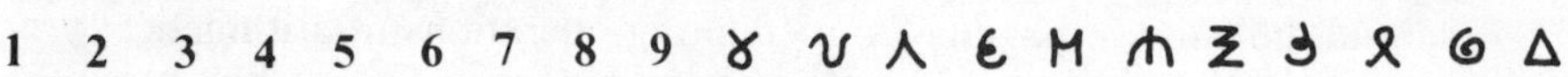

1 2 3 4 5 6 7 8 9 forthcoming

Figure 2.1

Clearly such a system would be unworkable in any culture that used numbers greater than a dozen or so. Arithmetic would be impossible since one could not, with the list given, have a product such as 3×9 without further symbols, since there is no symbol for 27.

Another way is to devise a repetitive scheme that enables one to count indefinitely with a limited set of words. The repetitive scheme produces a pattern, and this pattern, together with the symbols that express it, is the *notation*.

The number words themselves are constructed to a pattern of decades. There are irregularities in many languages which reflect earlier systems of counting in dozens or scores, but these settle down as the numbers get larger.

The decades are familiar,

    First decade   : one, two . . . up to ten
    Second decade : Twenty, thirty . . . up to a hundred
    Third decade   : Two hundred, three hundred . . . up to a thousand,
                 and so on.

Hence any number can be written down by using sufficient components.

Three hundred thousand two hundred and twenty-one is an example of such a compound.

The number words then enable any set to be counted and the result recorded. The next step is to pass from counting to computing. One can count a set of twenty-three objects and another set of fifty-nine but only computation gives the total without combining the two sets and beginning the count again.

In seeking a technique, antiquity hit on the device known as an abacus. Probably the earliest calculating technique was merely to combine and count piles of pebbles, and indeed the word calculation, from the Latin *calculus*, a small pebble, suggests this.

The abacus in its various forms used the device of exchange value, a device which is now embedded in our notation. Since its use eventually gave rise to the notation, its use in class as a lead up to notational studies is likely to be of value.

The first abacus seems to have been a smooth sand surface, with furrows made by the finger in parallel rows or columns. The user could count by putting pebbles into the first furrow, but only up to nine. On the count 'ten' the nine pebbles would be removed and one pebble to represent ten put in the second furrow. Thus five would be

Figure 2.2

and fifteen would be

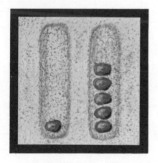

Figure 2.3

The Hindu mathematicians who developed the modern notation replaced the pebbles and grooves of the abacus by number symbols in columns.

If columns are ruled and the sets of pebbles replaced by the number symbols, the notation begins to emerge. In place of the compound number word, there is now a compound number symbol.

23

Thus one hundred and forty-three becomes on the abacus

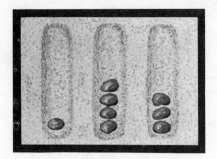

Figure 2.4

and in the position notation

| 1 | 4 | 3 | Figure 2.5

with the digits 1 and 4 representing one hundred and forty because of their position. On the abacus two hundred and three would be

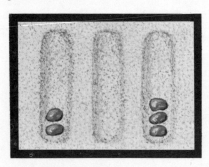

Figure 2.6

and in the symbolic notation

| 2 | | 3 | Figure 2.7

The introduction of a tenth symbol by the Arabs, the cypher or zero represented by 0, brought the notation to perfection by dispensing with the column. The zero showed that a column was to be left empty. In place of

| 1 | | | Figure 2.8
  ten

with the columns showing the value of the digit, ten could be written

10

and two hundred and three becomes 203. The zero thus introduced makes arithmetic as we know it possible.

3 Learning the notation

a Notational patterns

Since the place value notation gives rise to patterns in the structure of number symbols, there are two ways of learning it

    1 by direct study of place and exchange values,

    2 by investigating notational pattern in number.

The first is the traditional approach; the second is not only interesting in itself, but helps to bring out the structure of notation.

Note that some number patterns, such as the alternation of odd and even, are independent of the notation. Eight is an even number even if written as 13 (one three) in base 5. The simplest notational patterns arise directly from the decade structure. They are best seen from either the 100 square or the 100 track. The 100 track, often found mounted at a convenient height on a classroom wall, is a long strip divided into 100 equal parts, each clearly marked from 1–100. With the track go a number of shorter strips, several for each length from 1–10, correspondingly numbered. Tracks may be obtained commercially, may be made up from strips of graph paper, or, very satisfactorily, made by stretching out 100-cm tape measures. With these latter, children who use coloured arithmetic rods to a centimetre module do not need a supply of shorter strips, since they can use the rods.

One must note that two kinds of track are possible. In one the spaces are marked 1 2 3 . . . as on a block graph like this

1	2	3	4	5	6	

                                                     Figure 2.9

In the other the marks correspond to those on a ruler, like this

                                                     Figure 2.10

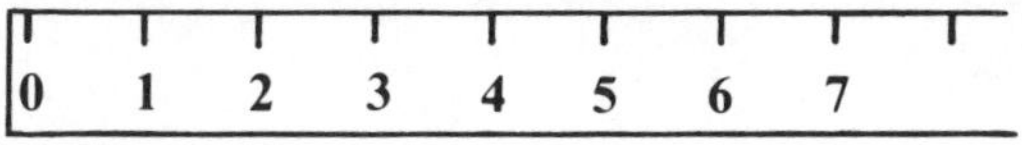

Children can learn to use either; the first, with numbered sections, corresponds to the basic counting process, but the second corresponds to the calibration of measuring instruments and shows another use for the symbol 0. On this type, zero marks, as on a measure, the *beginning* of the first interval, and we have the concept of zero as an *origin*. At first, the track merely displays the numbers up to 100, without emphasizing any notational pattern. It can then be used to illustrate addition by putting two short strips end to end; the sum of the numbers they represent is indicated by the position reached on the scale.

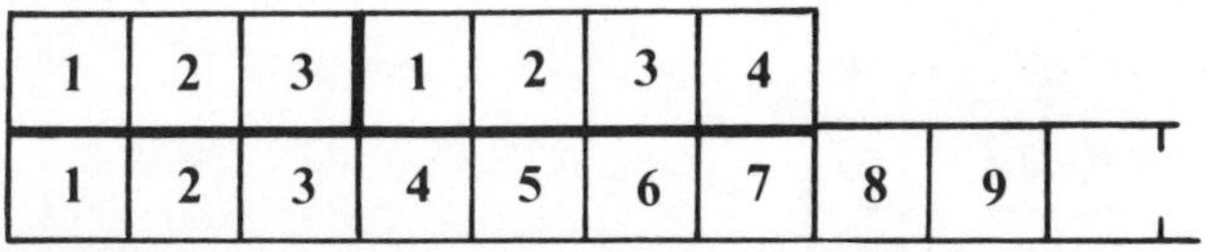

1	2	3	1	2	3	4			
1	2	3	4	5	6	7	8	9	

                                                     Figure 2.11

If the first strip is removed, it is seen that 4 can also be added to 3 by putting the beginning of the 4 strip after the mark 3 on the 100 track. This is important, since we can now progress along the track obtaining the sums in decades.

$$3+4=7 \qquad 13+4=17 \qquad 23+4=27 \qquad 33+4=37$$

When the structure of this process becomes clear to the child, so that without hesitation he can say $63+4=67$ because he has seen the pattern that is developing, he is probably ready for discussion of notation.

A similar demonstration is available for subtraction.

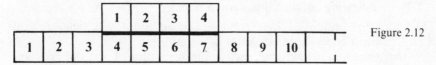

Figure 2.12

Working 'backwards' (note the convention of direction, accepted without question by the child) it can be seen that

$$7-4=3$$

and this is developed for higher decades, as before, to establish the pattern

$$17-4=13 \qquad 27-4=23 \qquad 37-4=33$$

Later, the pupil will meet the convention that movement or measurement from left to right is positive, from right to left negative. Work with the number track prepares him for this.

If addition and subtraction are done with piles of counters or shells, pupils are operating with 'unstructured' apparatus and the patterns of decades do not appear as readily as they do with the number track. This suggests the important point that any process should be demonstrated in as many ways and with as many different kinds of apparatus as possible. Each new approach carries a bonus of new insight.

The 100 square (or board) exhibits the decade patterns in a different way, since it arranges the numbers not on a line but in rows and columns of ten. It should be made accurately square with the numbers in square cells so that diagonal patterns can be established.

1	2	3	4	5	6	7	8	9	10
11	12	13	14	15	16	17	18	19	20
21	22	23	24	25	26	27	28	29	30
31	32	33	34	35	36	37	38	39	40
41	42	43	44	45	46	47	48	49	50
51	52	53	54	55	56	57	58	59	60
61	62	63	64	65	66	67	68	69	70
71	72	73	74	75	76	77	78	79	80
81	82	83	84	85	86	87	88	89	90
91	92	93	94	95	96	97	98	99	100

Figure 2.13

Possible activities would be

Write down all the numbers ending in 0.
Write down all the numbers beginning with 3.
Write down all the numbers ending with 5.

These and others are notation activities which help the child to grasp the structure of the patterns.

b Number bases

Once the pupil has begun to see the decade structure of the natural numbers as given by number tracks and 100 squares, he can begin a more detailed study of the notation.

The first step is to pass from heaps of counters to bundles, conveniently of straws or cocktail sticks. Thirty-seven sticks are put into three bundles of ten and a group of seven is left.

$37 = (3 \times 10) + 7$

The results can be tabulated for several numbers including the counts for which the singles are zero.

Bundles of ten	Singles
3	7
2	0
5	3

In this activity, each group of ten straws as it is counted out is bundled up and fastened with an elastic band. It can then be handled and put aside for counting as a single object. If several children have made their bundles, one can put them together and discuss the size of 'bundles of bundles'.

The next stage is a crucial one, since it makes the first move into abstraction. Instead of bundling the counting objects together, single objects are set aside to *represent* bundles. In the abacus this is done by using beads or pebbles arranged in columns, the position of the column designating a given bead as a single or a 'bundle' equivalent to ten singles.

There are four common forms of the abacus.

1 The sand tray already mentioned on page 23 using pebbles or beans.
2 A sheet of stiff paper folded to give two or three V-shaped grooves, also using pebbles.
3 A spike abacus of vertical wires on which beads can be put.
4 The hoop abacus, which obviates loose beads but keeps unused ones out of sight behind the partition.

Even if the last two are used for convenience in handling, children will like to see and handle the others, particularly the sand abacus which was possibly used in biblical times.

Sand tray abacus

Paper/pebble abacus

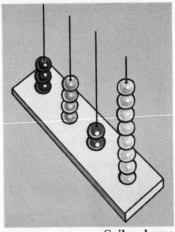

Spike abacus

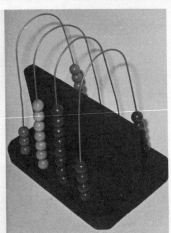

Hoop abacus

Using base ten, the beads on the first wire count singles up to 9, beads on the second wire count 10s up to 90, beads on the third wire count 100s and so on. Here for example is 324.

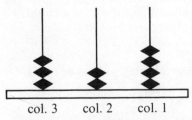

col. 3   col. 2   col. 1

Figure 2.14

An abacus can be used for any base by deciding at what number of beads exchange into the next column takes place, and children are often interested in trying out different bases. In practical terms, the value of our number system lies in its base ten structure common to all modern civilised societies; but work in other bases, kept within reasonable bounds, gives a useful insight into the nature of our number symbolism. It also makes clear that the choice of ten as a base is arbitrary.

Any one pattern of beads on an abacus will represent various numbers according to the base chosen. Consider this example.

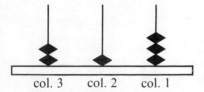

Figure 2.15

col. 3   col. 2   col. 1

If the base is 10 this represents

$(2 \times 100) + (1 \times 10) + 3$

normally written

213.

If, however, the base is 8, each bead on column 2 represents eight units, and each bead on column 3 represents (8×8) or 64 units.

Hence the abacus now shows

$(2 \times 64) + (1 \times 8) + 3.$

If this is written, counting the beads on each wire, the result is, as before,
213.

This at once introduces a difficulty that makes it necessary to approach multi-base arithmetic with caution. A pupil, or anyone else, will read this as 'two hundred and thirteen'. In fact the number of single beads represented is one hundred and thirty-nine.

Hence one must make it clear that the notation 213 is here working on an exchange rate of eight, and it could, therefore, be written

213 (eight)

One could then write

213 (eight) = 139 (ten)

The right-hand expression, although correct, appears to be an unnecessary complication, and probably the best way of settling the problem is to say that 213 (eight) represents a count of 139. It is then taken for granted that during a count base 10 is implied.

If pupils work with an abacus or multi-base blocks, they can overcome these difficulties. The configuration given could be on any other base, for example

base four: $(2 \times 16) + (1 \times 4) + 3$ or 213 (four) = 39 (ten)

base twelve: $(2 \times 144) + (1 \times 12) + 3$ or 213 (twelve) = 303 (ten)

In each case the convention adopted here is to represent the base by the number *word*, not the symbol.

The size of the number represented with the given beads increases as the base increases, but the number of symbols that need to be learned increases as well. To pass from an abacus base twelve to a column notation using symbols would need symbols for ten and eleven, since up to eleven beads can be put on the first

29

wire. These come off and are replaced by a bead on the second wire at twelve, and hence this number is given symbolically by

   10 (twelve)

This should be read as 'one zero'. It will be seen that 'one zero' represents the base number in *any* base.

If the base is small, more frequent exchanges have to be made, and hence more spikes or columns are needed. On a base two abacus one has to change at the second bead, so that the first few numbers appear as

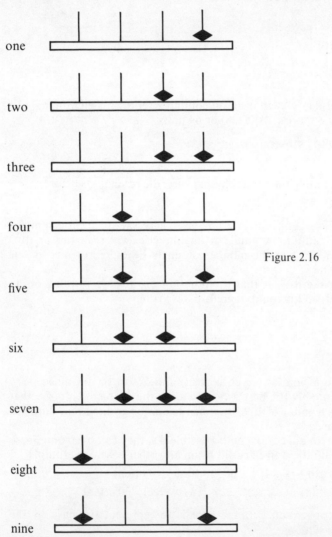

one

two

three

four

Figure 2.16

five

six

seven

eight

nine

In writing this base two notation, only the symbols 1 and 0 are needed, but more columns have to be used. Thus

   1001 (two)=9 (ten)

The exploration of the abacus can be paralleled by exchange operations using coloured counters. Any exchange values can be tried by the pupils, who will already be used to keeping tally with counters on a one-to-one correspondence with the objects counted. If it is decided that a blue counter is worth four yellows and a yellow four reds, then the blue, yellow and red counters can be used to keep tally, making the exchange as required. Discussion then allows the conclusion that a *fixed* exchange value is easier to handle. This fixed exchange value is the base of notation.

Example:

If 4 red counters count as 1 yellow,

4 yellow counters count as 1 blue,

then the set of letters in the alphabet

{a, b, c, d . . . z}

can be put into one-to-one correspondence with, initially, red counters. But when four red counters are down, they are exchanged for a yellow, and so on.

The final tally will be recorded by

1 blue   2 yellow   2 red

which is equivalent, on a base four abacus, to

Figure 2.17

and finally 122 (four) = 26 (ten)

Work with exchange values is suggested in class as the lead-in to notational study. Although work with the abacus and exchange values, particularly as a means of recording a count, can begin quite early, one would not extend the activity until most of the base ten number facts have been met and understood, even if not remembered.

4   Number facts and number patterns

Learning the number facts, that is, the sums, differences and products of the first few natural numbers, is a continuing process which will have accompanied the earlier work of this chapter. One cannot dispense with a knowledge of these facts, which are essential to the efficient use of number, and the sooner they are known the better.

A child who 'counts on' to arrive at $5+4=9$ does not *know* this fact; he merely knows a process for getting at it. It is also clear that a product such as

437×34 is not likely to be known, but one can *calculate* it if one knows the products 4×7, 3×3, 4×3, 4×4 and 3×7.

The list of required number facts is now usually taken as

1 sums and differences up to 20

2 products and quotients in the range $10 \times 10 = 100$.

These will be learnt gradually as the pupil passes through the early years of school.

When adding the digits to compute a sum such as $497 + 691$ the largest sum needed to be known is $9 + 9 = 18$, but it seems reasonable to go as far as 20. Three-digit facts are not required since addition proceeds in pairs. For example,

$$5 + 4 + 3 = 9 + 3$$
$$= 12$$

Note also that $19 + 3 = 22$ is not required as a simple fact, but is a notational concept. The fact needed is $9 + 3 = 12$. (See also page 26.)

At one time products were learnt up to 12×12 because of the requirements of Imperial measures and the currency, but these products are not required for denary or decimal algorithms and need not be taught.

The sum and difference facts will be learnt from very early work with conkers, beads, counters, or shells.

Multiplication, first introduced as continued addition, can arise when a single number strip is stepped out the required number of times along the track, as with

$$2 + 2 + 2 + 2 = 8$$

which is written

$$4 \times 2 = 8$$

Note the convention adopted here that 4×2 is read as 'four lots of two', so that the symbol $4 \times$ reads 'four lots of' or 'four groups of'. The other convention is that 4×2 is read as 'four multiplied by two', so that 4 is the multiplicand. The existence of the two conventions often causes difficulty at this stage. As the apparatus shows, 4×2 is numerically equal to 2×4, but this equivalence is rarely established early enough.

The first convention is the one used in algebra and later levels of mathematics, and can be established in class without comment.

If multiplication is thus seen as continuous addition, division then arises as continuous subtraction. The operations

$$8 - 2 - 2 - 2 - 2 = 0$$

are equivalent to

$$2 + 2 + 2 + 2 = 8$$

In words, four lots of two make up eight, and from a group of eight one can take four lots of two. Here the convention adopted is that this is written, $8 \div 2 = 4$, $\frac{8}{2} = 4$, or $8/2 = 4$. On this convention $\frac{8}{4} = 2$ states that 8 is made up with two groups of 4, or that one can remove a group of 4 from 8 twice before the group of eight is exhausted.

Mathematically, the pairs of operations, addition and subtraction, multiplication and division, are said to be *inverse* to one another. For addition

$8+2=10$ $\qquad$ $10-2=8$

If both are performed, the original number is unchanged

$(8+2)-2=8$

For multiplication

$4\times2=8$ $\qquad$ $\frac{8}{2}=4$ $\qquad$ and $(4\times2)\div2=4$

This gives the general meaning of an inverse process or operation; it is one that, applied after a given operation, restores the operand to its original value.

The phrases 'four groups of two' or 'four lots of two' tend to be tedious in use, and can be contracted to 'four twos'. For division the corresponding phrase for $8\div2$ is best left as 'eight divided by two', although it is explained as the question 'how many twos in eight?'. Explanations such as '$8\div2=4$ means how many times 2 goes into 8' are best avoided since they do not correspond to an actual operation.

Taking together each sum or product to be learnt with its inverse statement produces equivalent facts in sets of four.

Thus, for addition

 i $4+2=6$
 ii $2+4=6$
 iii $6-2=4$
 iv $6-4=2$

and for multiplication

 i $4\times2=8$
 ii $2\times4=8$
 iii $8\div4=2$
 iv $8\div2=4$

The first two in each set can be learnt together at the same time during the earliest stages, and are made clear, using the simplest materials, by setting them out like this:

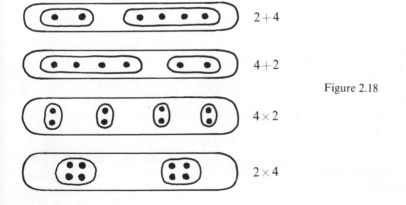

2+4

4+2

Figure 2.18

4×2

2×4

33

The traditional learning of tables requires each product to be memorized twice in isolation.

Once a start has been made on the number facts, a different approach may be begun. This takes the pupil into new paths for exploration, which only incidentally involve useful work in number facts. The topic suggested is that of number patterns, most of which are related to the notational system. The study of these patterns can be an early introduction to mathematical thinking as well as an incidental exercise in number.

A potentially rich situation is provided by the 100 square, which has already been mentioned as exhibiting clearly the patterns of the decades. Both blank and numbered squares are needed, and the work is most conveniently done on expendable duplicated sheets.

In general, the patterns are produced by repeating an operation until the square is full. Thus, on a blank square, the pupil can begin numbering the squares 1, 2, 3 . . . up to a chosen number. When he reaches this number, he does not write it in, but shades in the square instead. Numbering begins again at the next square, working from left to right as with writing, and once more the chosen square is shaded in. Here, as an example, is a blank 100 square, which has been partly filled and shaded to a count of 7.

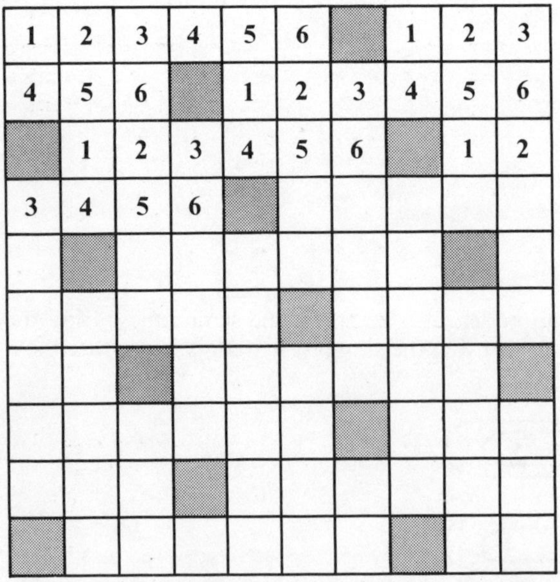

1	2	3	4	5	6	▓	1	2	3
4	5	6	▓	1	2	3	4	5	6
▓	1	2	3	4	5	6	▓	1	2
3	4	5	6	▓					
	▓							▓	
				▓					
		▓							▓
					▓				
			▓						
▓						▓			

Figure 2.19

It is very interesting to watch children do these exercises, and to note at what point a child will grasp the pattern and fill in the rest of the squares without bothering to count. He is more likely to do this if he is allowed to count without actually filling in the numbers, and he will probably mark the count with dots until the pattern is seen. Some children will enjoy producing and collecting these patterns systematically, and will be interested in trying a count to a number

34

greater than 10. They might also like to try patterns on blank squares other than 10×10. Here, as an example, is a 6×6 square shaded to a count of 5 (a count which shades vertical columns on a 10×10 square).

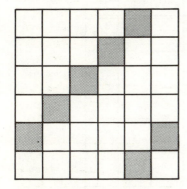

Figure 2.20

If this activity is transferred to a 100 square with the squares numbered as on page 26, the patterns then correspond to sets of multiples. On duplicated squares the numbers can be ringed or crossed through if the shading cannot be done lightly enough to leave them legible.

Thus to begin at 1 and cross out every second number thereafter gives a column pattern of the odd numbers; to start at two gives the pattern of the even numbers and also the multiples of two. The pattern of the count of seven now exhibits the multiples of seven,

> 7   14   21   28   . . . .

and these can, if the teacher wishes, be recorded as a table taken from the square,

$1 \times 7 = 7$
$2 \times 7 = 14$
$3 \times 7 = 21$
. . . . . .
. . . . . .
. . . . . .

If on one 100 square all the numbers are ringed to a count of three and then crossed through to a count of two, it will be seen that on some squares the patterns coincide. The numbers so marked form the pattern of the multiples of six.

This suggests a new stage in number knowledge: not only does the pupil learn products as such, but factors. If $4 \times 9 = 36$, then $36 = 4 \times 9$. The pattern does not, of course, give *prime* factors, but does let the pupil grasp the relation 'is a factor of' when it is set up between two numbers.

The products obtained need to be memorised and systematically recorded. An effective and useful way of doing this is to use the double entry multiplication square which gives the products in rows and columns. It can be given to the child as a blank with the border entries 1–10 filled in. The pupil can complete the square, using any methods that occur or can be suggested to him. It is not suggested that the pupil should merely copy a completed square. Here is a bordered multiplication square with a few entries.

×	1	2	3	4	5	6	7	8	9	10
1	1	2								
2		4								
3	3					18				
4										
5										
6						36				
7						42				
8									72	
9										
10							70			100

Figure 2.21

Once made, the square can be pasted on card and used for reference should any products be forgotten or unsure.

The square also shows a variety of patterns which are worth investigating for their own sake, which also give practice within a range of number facts. One sees that it is symmetrical about a diagonal from top left to bottom right, and pupils could be asked a number of questions to bring out its many other properties.

Typical questions would be

1 Do all the numbers from 1–100 appear?

2 How many numbers appear twice?

3 Do the numbers on the diagonals have special properties?

4 Is there anything to be said about numbers between 1–100 which do *not* appear?

5 Does a pattern appear if a number, say 12, is ringed each time it appears?

One can also generate patterns on this square which can be compared with those on the 100 square. Here, for example, is a 'plaid' pattern obtained by shading in the multiples of four.

1	2	3	4	5	6	7	8	9	10
2	4	6	8	10	12	14	16	18	20
3	6	9	12	15	18	21	24	27	30
4	8	12	16	20	24	28	32	36	40
5	10	15	20	25	30	35	40	45	50
6	12	18	24	30	36	42	48	54	60
7	14	21	28	35	42	49	56	63	70
8	16	24	32	40	48	56	64	72	80
9	18	27	36	45	54	63	72	81	90
10	20	30	40	50	60	70	80	90	100

Figure 2.22

The shaded rows and columns give the products in the tables of fours and eights; the other shaded numbers all have four as a factor. Teachers will also be interested in these investigations because they are self-regulating as between able and less able children. The teacher can always suggest another pattern to look for if any child finishes quicker than another.

If one asks why these patterns occur one sees that there are two distinct kinds. The first is notational, the second arises from the structure of the number system, which uses the operation $+1$ to relate each number to its successor, starting from 1 itself. Hence each second number is divisible by 2, each third by 3, each fourth by 4. This is a fundamental pattern of number independent of the notation. Other patterns, also independent of the notation, may be derived from this one.

For example, if there is a sequence of numbers, each 1 more than its predecessor, as

    42   43   44   45   46   47   48   49

and if each is divided by, say, 3, the remainders form the pattern

    0   1   2   0   1   2   0   1

This more difficult example is given to suggest that work with number is an 'open-ended' topic whose limits are set only by the ability of the investigator.

Other more sophisticated patterns are notational in origin, as the patterns of digits on the 100 square. An example might be of interest.

Since there is no single symbol for the word *ten* in the notation, it is written as 10, with 1 and the place holder 0. Then eleven becomes 11, twelve 12, thirteen 13 and so on. It follows that if the digits of the numbers 10, 11, 12, 13 . . . 18 are added together, they generate the numbers 1–9. Nineteen, written 19, now gives a two digit sum, 10; but if these digits are added, the final sum is $1+0=1$. It follows that, if the whole numbers are written down in order and their digits added, repeating the addition till only one digit is left, the pattern becomes

1   2   3   4   5   6   7   8   9   1   2   3   4   . . .

repeated indefinitely. This one-digit number is called the *digital root* of the original number. For example, the digital root of 887 is 5

since $8+8+7=23$ $2+3=5$

If a sequence of numbers forms a pattern, their digital roots form a pattern also.

Thus, if the products of 2 are tabulated from 1×2 to 18×2 together with the digital roots, this pattern emerges

Product	Digital root	Product	Digital root
2	2	20	2
4	4	22	4
6	6	24	6
8	8	26	8
10	1	28	1
12	3	30	3
14	5	32	5
16	7	34	7
18	9	36	9

There are corresponding patterns for all the tables of products. The above is given as an example of a notational pattern, but it is not a suggested class activity at this stage, although an experienced teacher could present it to pupils who have not yet learned computational skills.

There are some notational patterns which can be an aid to learning. The table of nines shows a structure

$1 \times 9 = 9$
$2 \times 9 = 18$
$3 \times 9 = 27$
$4 \times 9 = 36$
$5 \times 9 = 45$
· · · · · · · ·
· · · · · · · ·
· · · · · · · ·

38

An imaginative child could complete the table merely by continuing the pattern, increasing the tens digit and decreasing the units digit by one each time, so that the digital sum remains constant at 9.

5 Number games

Many teachers have a repertoire of number games which they use in class. If games are to be acceptable to the pupils, they must be worth playing and enjoyable in their own right. Some of the simpler ones are clearly intended to practise number facts, but others call for a strategy in addition to numerical expertise. Some of these are difficult for young children to play, while the simpler ones are not likely to maintain interest for long. There are also number activities which depend on constructing patterns but which can be put over as games if the teacher so wishes. A few examples follow.

The first has a definite strategy for winning, and can be organised as a class championship. The second is useful because it is flexible, since a suitable choice of process and numbers allows for a range of achievement. It is only suited to younger pupils.

Sixty-up

The digits 1–9 are written in a line on the blackboard. The two players take turns to point to a number, and a third child acts as the scorer, marking in a column on the board the cumulative total of the score. The first player to push the score to sixty is the *loser*. The game provides excellent number bond practice, particularly for the scorer. An obvious alternative is to begin with a number and to subtract the digit indicated; the loser is then the player who first reduces the total to zero.

Splash!

This is a good game for practising number bonds and products or quotients. There are nine (or ten or twelve) stepping stones in a river, marked in random order.

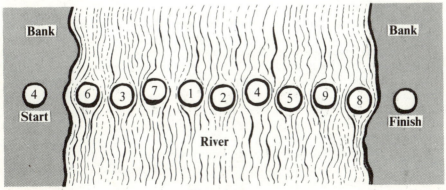

Figure 2.23

A process, multiplication for example, is decided on, a number is put in the 'start' box, a volunteer from the class then gives the products as he goes from stone to stone. If he gets a product wrong he has slipped into the water and the entire class calls 'Splash!'.

Activity number test

An activity based on the patterns that arise if a regular sequence of operations is performed on a set of numbers that already form a pattern, can also be presented as a game. It is a useful test that calls for a firm knowledge of number facts.

As presented by the teacher, the activity could be.

"Write down, across the page, the odd numbers from 1, until you reach the edge or until I say stop."

1	3	5	7	9	11

"Write down the even numbers from 2 underneath the others."

1	3	5	7	9	11
2	4	6	8	10	12

"Add the columns."

3	7	11	15	19	23

"Multiply each number by 6."

18	42	66	90	114	138

"Subtract 12 from each."

6	30	54	78	102	126

"Divide each by 2."

3	15	27	39	51	63

"Go along the line subtracting the first number from the second, the second from the third, and so on."

12	12	12	12	12

Then every child who has a line of twelves performed every operation correctly.

It is worth examining what has been done. First, if the word 'stop' is given as the quickest child reaches the edge of the paper, the slower children will have fewer numbers to deal with throughout the test, and should be able to keep up. In the example given, apart from distinguishing between odd and even numbers, the child has done six quick additions, has practised multiplications by six, has done six subtractions and six divisions by 2. And the entire exercise is automatically checked. All that the teacher need do is to see personally any child who does *not* get the row of twelves. No marking as such is necessary.

It should be seen that an indefinite number of tests of this kind can be devised by changing the numbers and the processes in the example given. Each is self-contained and can be done when a class or group is together with a few minutes to spare. Each test can be accepted by the pupils as a game, rather like the 'think of a number' trick.

6 Numerical statements

The concept of a factual statement is fundamental to language in one, but only one, of its aspects. A statement is used to state a fact, and it becomes true or false according to what is actually the case.

A horse has four legs is a true statement.

Pigs have wings is a false statement.

The language of mathematics is mainly made up of statements of this kind, usually expressed symbolically. Thus

$$3+2=5 \qquad 4-2=6$$

are examples of true and false statements.

There are, of course, many sentences in English which are not simple statements of fact, in so far as they express emotions, beliefs, attitudes or judgements of value.

"This book is not worth buying" is not a *factual* statement, however worth acting on, and, by and large, mathematics does not try to deal with such statements directly, in spite of their practical importance. Besides being true or false, statements also exist in a form one can call *incomplete*.

"Three and two make" is an incomplete statement, made true by adding the word *"five"* and false by adding any other number word. If a word other than a number word is added, the statement ceases to be of any use to the mathematician, and he calls it a badly-formed statement or refuses it any meaning.

"Three and two make green" is such a meaningless statement. On the other hand, a statement known to be false is often useful. If one arrives at the result $3+2=6$ one knows that an argument has gone wrong or that a process is not working properly.

The child learning his number facts may not realize that he is making statements that obey the normal rules of English. He can be helped by having the demand for numerical information in the form of an incomplete statement which he is required to complete. The situation has been put into an easily handled schema by using the 'place-holder' notation.

This forms a simple notation, but at the same time a very powerful teaching aid. Instead of leaving a gap in the number statement, one puts a shape into which the number can be inserted. This can be any shape at all, but obviously something that is easily drawn is most convenient and the shapes usually found are $\square$ and $\triangle$.

This 'place-holder' (usually read as 'box' or 'triangle' according to shape) goes in place of the number or numbers which are missing.

The first use of the place-holder should be simple examples of the type $3+\square=5$. And the question one asks is, "What number or numbers do we put in the box to make this statement true?" For instance, if one puts 3 in the box, the statement is 'false'. This approach is important later when dealing with equations with more than one solution and with identities.

This simple device can be used for developing all kinds of number patterns. For example,

$$3+\square=5 \qquad 13+\square=15 \qquad 23+\square=25 \qquad \text{and so on.}$$

As with the number track patterns given on pages 25 and 26, the track is a valuable aid in completing the statements.

All the related statements using the other operations can also be introduced, but only as the children extend their knowledge of number facts:

$$5-\square=3 \qquad 5\times\square=15 \qquad 10\div\square=2 \qquad \text{and so on.}$$

Since the incomplete statement can be interpreted as a question, it is reasonable to use the word 'answer' in referring to the numbers that can be inserted. It then makes sense to say that

$$3+2=\square$$

has one and only one answer that makes it true but an indefinite number that make it false. By using the symbols

$$< \text{ less than} \qquad > \text{ greater than}$$

statements can be offered for consideration that have several or an indefinitely large number of true answers, so that one can speak of a set of answers, or 'answer set'. For example

$$3+\square <8 \text{ gives the answer set } \{0, 1, 2, 3, 4\}$$

This result, of course, assumes that fractions are excluded. Similarly

$$3+\square=2$$

has *no* answers if the discussion is restricted to the ordinary numbers used for counting. The set of all answers is *null* (see page 21). It is possible to vary the position occupied by the place-holder. Thus

$$3+\square=5 \qquad \square+2=5 \qquad 3+2=\square$$

represent the same statement when completed but each calls for a different number to occupy it.

At a later stage, after number facts are grasped confidently, the use of the notation can be extended to more than one place-holder. A statement for completion could be

$$\square+\triangle=6$$

This is now a more complicated structure, and really needs tabulated results to make it clear.

$\square$	$\triangle$
0	6
1	5
2	4
3	3
4	2
5	1
6	0

It is introduced here to show the scope of the notation, which can be used from early stages in number work, but remains useful at higher levels. It allows work to begin in primary schools that introduces important concepts from the area of mathematics usually known as algebra.

Chapter 3

THE APPROACH TO COMPUTATION

1 Computation and algorithms

Computation depends on knowledge of the number facts. The product of 6 and 3 is known, but the product of 216 and 73 is not. Computation is the process whereby such results as $216 \times 73 = 15768$ are obtained, and the set of rules used is called an *algorithm*. There are algorithms for all the processes of arithmetic. In the past the teaching of algorithms was often the main content of school mathematics.

Various algorithms for the Four Rules have been developed over the past few centuries, and all agree that a pupil needs to acquire an efficient set that will serve any likely calls on his computational skill.

There are two points to be made.

1 Algorithms are invented processes for arriving at results, and are to be judged in terms of efficiency and convenience.

2 Algorithms call for a prior knowledge of the number facts as given in Chapter 2. They work by manipulating the notation using this knowledge.

It follows that work with computation should be delayed until the pupil has a firm grasp of number facts and has begun to understand the notation. It should be possible to arrive at a provisional algorithm step by step, with each step explicable in terms of the notation. The algorithm thus obtained may not be compact and rapid, but it has more chance of being understood and is less subject to error; so that for the beginner it is more efficient.

Such preliminary algorithms are called *extended algorithms* because each step is set out in full. A good extended algorithm is one that can later be contracted to a standard algorithm. It should also present a neat array of symbols so that the process can be traced and sources of error discovered.

Extended algorithms are essentially teaching algorithms. A slower pupil who just manages to cope with them may delay or never reach the contracted methods, but as children grow in competence they begin to grow out of the extended forms. Only exceptional children are likely to see for themselves the contracted forms and sooner or later the efficient methods need to be demonstrated and practised. The teacher, of course, decides at what stage the changeover should be made. Algorithms are not unique processes and many more are possible than ever appear in schools.

For most children at primary level the use of quotients obtained by a formal division algorithm is rarely needed. In any case the algorithm for long division is rather difficult, and, if used at all, might well be given only to the very able child. It is discussed here as an extended algorithm for the sake of completeness, although it is not recommended for general teaching.

Moreover, even at the inverse product level, the teaching of division has always been troubled by the familiar fact that it corresponds to two distinct physical processes, the so-called subtractive and sharing aspects of division.

If I give three sweets to each child from this bag containing 27, how many children can I treat?

If I share this bag of 27 sweets equally among 3 children, how many does each get?

Although this physical distinction is clear enough and must be seen by the child – who should indeed at a very early stage familiarize himself with it by sharing out bags of conkers or beans – it remains that the actual formal algorithm is subtractive. As the inverse of multiplication (which is repeated addition) division appears in arithmetic as repeated subtraction, a fact more clearly seen in the operation of a mechanical desk calculator which performs the division by subtracting 3 from 27 until there is no remainder.

2 Addition

The sum of two one-digit integers is not in the ordinary sense of the word subject to computation, but is known as a number fact. The sum of two three-digit numbers is not usually known, but can be calculated. The result is found by applying the number facts to the notational structure. As an illustration, the columns can be represented by bundles of sticks or beads on an abacus, as discussed on page 27. Thus, for $47 + 36$

	bundles of ten	singles
	4	7
	3	6
Adding the singles gives	1	3
Adding the bundles gives	7	0
Total represented	8	3

This suggests the extended algorithm in which each column is dealt with separately, without a carrying figure.

$$
\begin{array}{r}
47 \\
+36 \\
\hline
13 \\
70 \\
\hline
83 \\
\end{array}
\qquad
\begin{array}{l}
7+ 6=13 \\
40+30=70 \\
\text{Total } =83
\end{array}
$$

Each stage calls for a number fact relating a pair of numbers to their sum. The knowledge that 4 tens + 3 tens = 7 tens is an extension of the basic fact 4+3=7, using the decade structure.

Numbers of three or more digits can be dealt with in a similar way.

$$
\begin{array}{r}
423 \\
+278 \\
\hline
\end{array}
$$

$$
\begin{array}{rcrcr}
11 & \qquad & 3+ & 8= & 11 \\
90 & & 20+ & 70= & 90 \\
600 & & 400+ & 200= & 600 \\
\hline
\end{array}
$$

$$
\begin{array}{rcrcr}
1 & & & & \\
100 & \qquad & 10+ & 90= & 100 \\
600 & & & & \\
\hline
701 & & & &
\end{array}
$$

Prolonged practice with the extended algorithm using numbers of three or more digits is not likely to be of value. What *is* desirable is that children should write out the algorithm for two-digit numbers until they are quite familiar with it and see for themselves how it can be contracted; how the process of bundling up ten of the singles for 'carrying over' to the next column can be represented on paper.

$$
\begin{array}{r}
47 \\
+36 \\
\hline
83 \\
\hline
{\scriptstyle 1}
\end{array}
$$

At first, children could be expected to explain what they are doing verbally by saying, for example, "7+6=13, put down 3 and carry one ten: 40+30=70 and 10 makes 80". They should not be taught to say "7+6=13, put down 3 and carry one: 4+3=7 and 1 is 8". This last is a permissible contraction, especially if one is adding numbers of many digits (population statistics, for example) but it should arise only after the familiarity of use. Once the pupil can add rapidly and accurately, the carrying digit can be omitted altogether and the algorithm becomes a mental one. All that appears on paper is

$$
\begin{array}{r}
47 \\
+36 \\
\hline
83
\end{array}
$$

This stage should not be hurried, and many primary children will never reach it. Children should also realize that numbers can be added in any order, or taken in pairs as convenient if there are more than two numbers. For example,

$$
27+33=33+27
$$
$$
(15+4)+32=15+(4+32)
$$

These facts need to be discussed in class and the children's attention drawn to them.

3   Subtraction

In the discussion of number facts which formed part of Chapter 2, subtraction was seen as the inverse process to addition, and it was suggested that number bonds could be learnt for differences as well.

$$8-3=5$$

then becomes a known fact and an algorithm for subtraction might suggest itself as simply

$$\begin{array}{r} 67 \\ -43 \\ \hline \end{array}$$

4	$7-\ 3=\ 4$
20	$60-40=20$
—	
24	Total $=24$

This contracts easily into

$$\begin{array}{r} 67 \\ -43 \\ \hline 24 \\ \hline \end{array}$$

Difficulties are avoided by choosing suitable examples, just as later the choice of $63-27=36$ serves to introduce the point at which subtraction becomes more complicated.

The various algorithms devised for dealing with this case are a sticking point for both teachers and pupils. An algorithm can often be constructed by considering a physical process involving numbers and recording the steps. Consider $63-27=36$. This result can be obtained from a pile of 63 counters by removing 27 and counting the remainder, but this process does *not* generate an algorithm because it does not correspond to anything in the notation. If the counters are replaced with 6 bundles of ten straws and 3 singles, the model does correspond, and a possible process for extracting 27 straws can be considered. One way is to withdraw 2 bundles of ten and the 3 single straws as a first step. Then a bundle is broken up into a pile of singles, 4 are removed to make the total taken to 27, leaving 3 bundles of ten and 6 single straws. This is not necessarily the most efficient way of handling the straws, but it leads to the required result and gives rise to an algorithm.

63	given $60+3$
-23	remove $20+3$
40	
$-\ 4$	remove 4 more
36	result $63-27$

This is now an extended algorithm for subtraction. It does not correspond to one of the standard methods used in schools, but it records neatly the steps in an actual process discussed. The number facts required are those arising from the decade patterns already established in Chapter 2, and it is given as an example of the construction of a workable method. It has the big disadvantage that the $+27$ being subtracted does not appear anywhere in the algorithm and needs to be stored mentally during the computation.

One can try another approach. This time, since there are not enough single straws, a bundle is broken up to give 10 extra, leaving 5 bundles untouched. The 7 straws can now be taken from the $10+3$, the 2 bundles of ten from the 5 bundles. A table showing the bundles and singles during the process now becomes

	bundles	singles	
	5	10	
6 bundles reduced to 5	6̸	3 }	total 13
	2	7	(7 from 10 is 3 and 3 gives 6)
	3	6	

This now gives a workable algorithm

$$
\begin{array}{cc}
{\scriptstyle 5} & {\scriptstyle 10} \\
6̸ & 3 \\
-2 & 7 \\
\hline
3 & 6 \\
\hline
\end{array}
$$

which corresponds to the decomposition method, so called because the notation 6 tens and 3 is decomposed into 5 tens and 13. Note that the ten taken from the tens column is written in full. It is also easier to say "7 from 10, 3; 3 and 3 is 6" than to say "10 and 3, 13; 7 from 13, 6". An advantage of the method is that the notation is adjusted in advance of the actual subtraction, which then is straight-forward. A possible disadvantage is that the deleted digit looks untidy, but even here, provided that the deletion is a single light dash, all the numerals in the algorithm are set out for inspection. Some teachers may prefer the notation

$$
\begin{array}{cc}
{\scriptstyle 5} & \\
6̸ & 13 \\
-2 & 7 \\
\hline
3 & 6 \\
\hline
\end{array}
$$

but this should be regarded as a contraction, adopted after the full decomposition is recorded.

The decomposition also corresponds to what one actually does if 1p has to be given, say, to each of 9 children from a purse containing two 10p coins and three 1p coins. One would actually change one 10p coin for ten 1p coins. The correspondence, although of practical importance in handling money, is not complete because the 10p coin is not composed of ten 1p coins, but is merely a token given that value by law.

Algorithms can also be derived from operations with an abacus.

Here is 63 on an abacus.

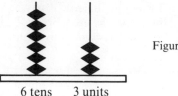

Figure 3.1

6 tens   3 units

47

Here is the same number decomposed.

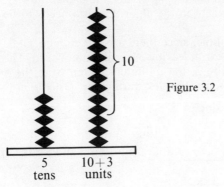

Figure 3.2

5	10+3
tens	units

Subtraction of 27 now corresponds to removing 7 unit beads and 2 tens beads from their columns, leaving

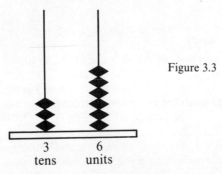

Figure 3.3

3	6
tens	units

Another common algorithm for subtraction is known as the equal addition method. It operates by adding one ten to both numbers, but decomposed as 10 units in the top line thus

$$
\begin{array}{cc}
t & u \\
6 & |3 \\
-2 & 7 \\
\end{array}
$$

becomes

$$
\begin{array}{cc}
t & u \\
6 & 13 \\
-3 & 7 \\
\hline
3 & 6 \\
\end{array}
$$

since the difference between the adjusted numbers is unchanged. Three points are worth noting. Firstly, the rigmarole "7 from 3 won't go, borrow 1, pay back the 1" does not fit the facts of the process and should never be used. Secondly, it is harder to explain than the decomposition method, and as commonly written

$$
\begin{array}{cc}
6 & {}_1 3 \\
-2_1 & 7 \\
\hline
\end{array}
$$

it only too easily becomes a rote-learned method. Thirdly, and most importantly, it does not correspond to a practical situation in handling money, the abacus, bundles of straws and other apparatus, and cannot readily be demonstrated with their help. The decomposition process merely rearranges the numbers within the notation; the other actually changes their value. The method is not recommended by the authors, but many schools use it.

There is a third and much more sophisticated method, which, dependent on mental skill and knowledge of the number bonds up to 20, is scarcely an algorithm at all, since it writes the answer without intermediate working or adjustment. This is the method of complementary addition, also called the Italian method from its Florentine origins in the seventeenth century. It is the extension to two or more digits of the process which, for example, replaces

$$7-2=\square \quad \text{by} \quad 2+\square=7$$

Instead of filling the $\square$ by asking what is 7 less 2, one fills it by saying "2 and 5, 7", that is, one replaces a subtraction fact by the complementary addition fact. Subtraction can now be set down directly exactly as on page 45.

$$
\begin{array}{cc}
6 & 7 \\
-4 & 3 \\
\hline
2 & 4
\end{array}
$$

The difference is in the mental step only; instead of saying "3 from 7, 4" one would say "3 and 4, 7", setting down the 4 in both cases.

If, however, one has

$$
\begin{array}{cc}
6 & 3 \\
-2 & 7
\end{array}
$$

the mental steps are more difficult and need explanation. One cannot make 7 up to 3 by addition, of course, so one makes it up to 13, saying "7 and 6, 13" and setting down the 6. The addition has thus produced a carrying figure, exactly as in two column addition, so the next addition is with 3 not 2, and one says, "3 and 3, 6", setting down the 3. The recorded calculation shows no working

$$
\begin{array}{cc}
6 & 3 \\
-2 & 7 \\
\hline
3 & 6
\end{array}
$$

The ten carried is not set down; it is assumed that only pupils well used to contracted addition without recording carrying digits would use this method. It is very rapid and accurate, but, because it cannot be done slowly a step at a time and recorded as an extended algorithm, it is not a good initial teaching method. One would hope that more able pupils would come to it later on.

A note on symbols

When addition and subtraction sums are given as isolated numerical exercises, the use of the $+$ or $-$ sign as in

$$
\begin{array}{cc}
24 & 26 \\
+32 & -14
\end{array}
$$

is probably advisable. Where calculations occur in context as part of the solution of problems, as most calculations should do after their early stages, the signs are probably redundant. One should avoid the notation

36—
17

as it is no part of the meaning of the minus sign to stand for 'this is a subtraction sum'.

4 Multiplication

The algorithm for multiplication extends products to numbers of two or more digits where it is no longer possible to rely on simple number facts. It depends on three principles, which can be illustrated using simple examples and then formally stated.

Example 1

$$4 \times 3 = 3 \times 4 \quad \text{and} \quad 24 \times 23 = 23 \times 24$$

This illustrates the so-called commutative law for products. Chapter 2 suggests that product pairs should be learnt in this way.

Example 2

$$4 \times (3+2) = (4 \times 3) + (4 \times 2)$$
$$= 12 + 8$$
$$= 20$$
$$\text{and } 4 \times 23 = 4 \times (20+3)$$
$$= (4 \times 20) + (4 \times 3)$$
$$= 80 + 12$$
$$= 92$$

This law is not easy to express in words informally, but in technical terms is given as *multiplication is distributive over addition*. It is very easily demonstrated by coloured rods.

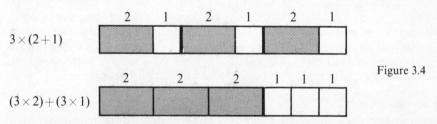

Figure 3.4

Children can be shown such configurations informally, without discussion of the laws as such, and will profit from setting out a number of products in this way before going on to the usual algorithm. Teachers will note that brackets are used here to link together parts of a longer statement. Their use can be shown to children more easily than described in words.

Example 3

$10 \times 23 = 230$

This example illustrates the fundamental process that arises in the notation when a number is multiplied by the base number (in this case ten), that is, the digits are moved one column to the left. The result is true for any number of digits. The zero appears as the place-holder to mark the units column now left empty.

The abacus illustrates the process very clearly.

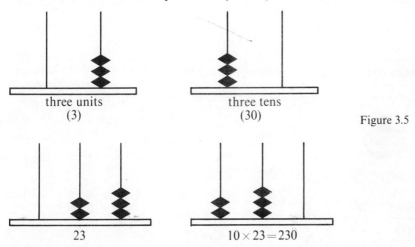

three units
(3)

three tens
(30)

Figure 3.5

23

$10 \times 23 = 230$

Once children have grasped the process of forming products with ten, the pattern of the decades takes them forward to such results as

$3 \times 20 = 60$ $30 \times 20 = 600$ $30 \times 3 = 90$

What must be avoided is the erroneous 'to multiply by ten add zero'. This is most unfortunate in that it gives the correct numerical form for integers, so that children readily accept it. It breaks down completely when work on decimals is begun and once taught remains a blockage that some pupils never clear away.

The algorithm for multiplication that can now be given depends on the distributive law and the decade pattern taken together. Set out formally in full as an example

$$34 \times 23 = 4(20+3) + 30(20+3)$$
$$= (80+12) + (600+90)$$
$$= 92 + 690$$
$$= 782$$

This now gives a simple extended algorithm for multiplication by one digit

```
    23
 ×   4
 ───────
    12      4 × 3
    80      4 × 20
 ───────
    92
 ───────
```

and an algorithm for multiplication by two or more digits also set out in full in the example

$$\begin{array}{r} 23 \\ \times 34 \\ \hline \end{array}$$

12	4×3
80	4×20
90	30×3
600	30×20
782	

It would be advisable for children to set out the algorithms as shown, and only when confident and proficient with this form should they begin to contract.

The contraction could proceed in two stages, firstly omitting the analysis. Thus

$$\begin{array}{r} 23 \\ \times 34 \\ \hline 12 \\ 80 \\ 90 \\ 600 \\ \hline 782 \end{array}$$

and then passing into its final contraction

$$\begin{array}{r} 23 \\ \times 34 \\ \hline 92 \\ 690 \\ \hline 782 \end{array}$$

which is the familiar form.

For the very good reason that the first partial product acts as a first approximation to the answer, many teachers prefer to multiply by the tens digit first. The algorithm then becomes

$$\begin{array}{r} 23 \\ \times 34 \\ \hline 690 \\ 92 \\ \hline 782 \end{array}$$

but the order of the analysis then becomes less clear. It is then

$$\begin{array}{r} 23 \\ \times\,34 \\ \hline \end{array}$$

90	30×3
600	30×20
12	4×3
80	4×20

$$\overline{782}$$

since the one-digit multiplication always begins from the right. One would, provisionally, recommend the first form with the other introduced by discussion later, perhaps at a secondary stage.

5 Division

The division facts appear in number work as the inverses of the products.

$9 \times 3 = 27$

Hence

$27 \div 9 = 3 \qquad 27 \div 3 = 9$

Many teachers prefer to replace the $\div$ symbol by a vinculum or an oblique stroke, e.g. $\frac{27}{9}$ or 27/9. The division facts can be learnt most readily by using the $\square$ notation, starting from products such as

$9 \times \square = 27$

Whether an algorithm is taught or not, full practice in inverse products is needed. This would include writing equivalent statements such as those on page 33, statements for completion using the box notation such as

$54 \div \square = 9 \qquad 35 \div 7 = \square$

and practice in writing such statements as problems.

Use of the 100 strip to show products and their inverses also helps the pupil to see why remainders occur in division.

$3 \times 7 = 21$ and so in $21 \div 3 = \square$

the number that fills the box *must* be 7.

But

$23 \div 3 = \square$

cannot be completed using whole numbers, because $3 \times \square = 23$ is not a true statement for any integer, since 7 leaves the product too small and 8 makes it too large.

Counting back in threes from 23 on a 100 strip shows the remainder clearly, and the pupil can write

$23 \div 3 = 7$ (rem. 2)

These statements can be practised and also interpreted as problems.

In schools that teach the algorithm, long division will probably appear as

$$
\begin{array}{r}
481 \\
12 \overline{)\ 5774} \\
48 \\
\hline
97 \\
96 \\
\hline
14 \\
12, \\
\hline
2
\end{array}
$$

Considerable contraction has occurred in this example. The starting question is usually taken as, "How many 12s in 57", but this is a contraction for "How many groups of twelve can be taken from 57 *hundred* to the nearest *hundred*?". The answer is found by multiplying up to reach the required number.

Set out in full the division now reads

$$
\begin{array}{r}
481 \\
\hline
1 \\
80 \quad \left. \right\} \text{ partial quotients added} \\
400 \\
12 \overline{)\ 5774} \\
4800 \qquad 400 \times 12 \\
\hline
974 \\
960 \qquad 80 \times 12 \\
\hline
14 \\
12 \qquad 1 \times 12 \\
\hline
2
\end{array}
$$

There is no logical reason why the largest possible subtrahend should be formed at each stage. Children often fill the side of the page (or odd scraps of paper if the teacher objects to visible working!) with multiplications to arrive at the correct partial quotient. Obviously, children should be encouraged to take away the largest group possible, but it is not *wrong* if they do not succeed in finding it the first time, and probably the insight they get into the process of successive approximation, quite unformulated at this stage, is well worth the extra lines of figuring in the final algorithm.

Here is the division done in this way

```
            481
         ─────
            1   ⎫
           20   ⎪
           60   ⎬  partial quotients added
          100   ⎪
          300   ⎭
        ─────
    12 ) 5774
        3600        300 × 12
        ─────
        2174
        1200        100 × 12
         ────
         974
         720         60 × 12
         ───
         254
         240         20 × 12
         ───
          14
          12          1 × 12
          ──
           2
```

Giving the final result

$5774 \div 12 = 481$ (rem. 2).

Because the occasions on which long division arises naturally in the applications of arithmetic to classroom situations are so few, there is very little call for the contracted algorithm, and this could well be left till a secondary stage. Initially, contraction would be the omission of the trial products, so that the algorithm becomes

```
            481
          ─────
            1
           80
          400
         ─────
    12 ) 5774
        4800
        ─────
         974
         960
         ───
          14
          12
          ──
           2
```

The partial quotients could then be condensed, so that it becomes

```
        481
12 ) 5774
     4800
     ────
      974
      960
     ────
       14
       12
      ───
        2
```

One would not recommend further contraction in the primary school.

6 Computation with decimals

This chapter is not concerned with the teaching of the decimal notation as such, but with its implication for computation. Taken as an extension of the notation for integers, the four processes of addition and subtraction with multiplication and division by integers carry over directly into decimals. The algorithms are modified only by the inclusion of the decimal point.

Using bundles and straws, the notation can be represented by cutting a single straw into ten parts.

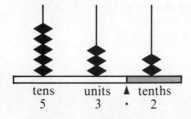

Figure 3.6

tens	units	▲ tenths
5	3	· 2

On the abacus the transition from units to tenths can be shown by a change in bead colour, a partition or by lines marked on the base. In the notation, the separator is the decimal point.

Using bundles and straws, the notation can be represented by cutting a single straw into ten parts.

bundles of ten	singles	tenths
5	3 ·	2

separator

Addition and subtraction

The extended algorithm for addition is now, to take an example,

```
  4·7
+ 3·6
```

| 1·3 | since 0·7+0·6=1·3 |
| 7·0 | since 4+3 =7 |

8·3

The points should appear in each partial sum and must be ranged one below the other, otherwise the place values are not defined clearly. To avoid confusion or mistake a decimal fraction with no units preferably carries a zero. Seven tenths is better written 0·7 not ·7. Many errors in use occur because this is not done and the point gets lost. In effect, the zero gives additional warning. Since the zero occupies a place, it helps alignment of the other digits.

```
   0·3
+ 36·1
```

36·4

If it is required to do so, the algorithm contracts exactly as before.

Subtraction also uses the algorithm for integers, but in the example, it is a unit which is decomposed into 10 tenths, not a ten into 10 units.

```
 5 10
 6·3
-2·7
```

3·6

Whenever numbers are written in columns and include both decimals and integers, it is advisable to use the zero in the tenths column for integers. Thus

```
 5 10
 6·0
-2·7
```

3·3

Multiplication and division

The basic step of multiplication by ten has the same effect on a decimal as on an integer; it shifts each digit one place to the left. The tenths multiplied by ten become units, and thus move to the next column.

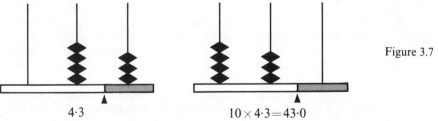

4·3   10 × 4·3 = 43·0

Figure 3.7

57

It is at this stage that children who have been taught the inappropriate rule "to multiply by 10 add zero" find themselves in difficulties, since they want to write $10 \times 4 \cdot 3 = 4 \cdot 30$ and often do.

Note that $10 \times 4 \cdot 3$ is written as $43 \cdot 0$ rather than 43 to remind the calculator that he is dealing with decimals. The zero here is not 'added', it stands in place of the empty tenths column for reference.

It follows that division by 10 shifts all digits one place to the *right*. Each column is reduced to one tenth of its original value, so that the 'tens' beads of an abacus become units beads on this representation. The units, divided into ten parts, become tenths and so the decimal separator is called into play and $43 \div 10 = 4 \cdot 3$. Pupils must become used to adding this point when needed. The rule "to divide by 10 insert a point" is misleading and should be avoided. The point goes after the units digit, and is not required if there are no fractional parts. Using examples, set out in full as extended algorithms, the two basic moves in multiplication and division become

$$
\begin{array}{c}
4 \cdot 3 \\
0 \cdot 3 \\
4 \cdot 0 \\
\end{array}
$$

$$
\begin{array}{rl}
 & 4 \cdot 3 \\
\times & 10 \\
\hline
 & 3 \cdot 0 \qquad 10 \times 0 \cdot 3 \\
 & 40 \cdot 0 \qquad 10 \times 4 \cdot 0 \\
\hline
 & 43 \cdot 0 \\
\end{array}
\qquad
\begin{array}{r}
10 \overline{)\, 43 \cdot 0} \\
40 \cdot 0 \qquad 10 \times 4 \cdot 0 \\
\hline
3 \cdot 0 \\
3 \cdot 0 \qquad 10 \times 0 \cdot 3 \\
\hline
\end{array}
$$

These examples analyse fully the process of multiplication and division involving numbers of more than one digit. They would normally occur as simple statements

$$4 \cdot 3 \times 10 = 43$$
$$43 \div 10 = 4 \cdot 3$$

but these forms imply all that has been discussed above.

There still remains one very important comment. The quotient $43 \div 10$ has been shown to be $4 \cdot 3$. Other quotients such as $8 \div 4 = 2$ are learnt as number facts, demonstrable by operations with counters. But the division algorithm as such uses products, not quotients. In general, a statement such as

$$8 \div 4 = \square$$

is completed by considering the inverse statement

$$\square \times 4 = 8$$

and the quotient in the long division algorithm is arrived at by using a programme of multiplication and subtraction. The process of division by ten discussed above is not in fact used in either the extended or contracted algorithms as given, but it is nevertheless fundamental in the notation and must be understood before confidence in using decimals can be reached.

Products involving decimals obey the rules of commutativity and distribution already formulated for integers, so that the final extended algorithms for the

58

two processes can be given at once. Using examples, multiplication can be set out as

```
      2·3
   × 34
   ─────
      1·2      4 × 0·3
      8·0      4 × 2·0
      9·0     30 × 0·3
     60·0     30 × 2·0
   ─────
     78·2
```

Long division with decimals is best not attempted in the primary school, but would be in the form

```
         48·1
        ─────
          0·1
          8·0
         40·0
        ─────
   12 ) 577·2
        480·0       40·0 × 12
        ─────
         97·2
         96·0        8·0 × 12
        ─────
          1·2
          1·2        0·1 × 12
```

Both could be contracted if necessary, but only after full understanding is reached. The division example differs from the earlier example with integers in that the final digit has been chosen to give an exact quotient without remainder. The treatment of the remainder in decimal division introduces new higher level concepts altogether, and should be delayed.

7 A note on the use of apparatus

Teachers are, inevitably, aware of the huge range of commercial number apparatus on the market designed to aid the teaching of computation. In this chapter apparatus has only been introduced to give a physical illustration to number processes, or to suggest algorithms for completing them.

Any apparatus which succeeds in demonstrating the notational process could well prove more convenient than the bundles of straws or simple forms of the abacus actually mentioned. Different forms of apparatus may even suggest different algorithms. Algorithms in their final form, accepted as standard methods, invariably imply the short-cutting of the steps that lead to their construction. The best apparatus is the one that shows each of these steps most clearly, and the best algorithm for the learner is the one that records each of these steps most fully. Apparatus, it is recommended, should be used freely at the teacher's discretion, but never to bypass the development of the algorithms. Apparatus gives a concrete representation of numerical processes, but the extended algorithms display the inner structure of computation.

Chapter 4

MONEY AND MEASURE

1 The nature of measurement

The stages by which cultures acquire the concept of measure seem clear, and are of importance to the teacher whose task is to help children who need to learn them. At first objects are merely described as big, small, hard and so on. Then the concept of comparison emerges, and one object is seen as bigger or longer or brighter than another. Finally, in an attempt to answer questions such as, "How big?" "How much longer?" the technique common to all measurement emerges; a standard is set up and the attributes are compared with this on a numerical scale.

The history of measurement shows two distinct lines of development, both of which are important for teaching:

1 the gradual spread of 'standardization' in producing precise and widely accepted units of measure;

2 the extension of the number of attributes that are regarded as capable of being measured by devising suitable standards and techniques of comparison.

Measure first began with man's own dimensions as the standard – the span, foot, cubit, inch, pace and mile are all familiar examples of such units. Later, these measures were standardized nationally or regionally by setting up legal definitions of them. At the time of the French Revolution an attempt was made to set up a connected system of units for all purposes. This, the metric system, developed gradually throughout the nineteenth century, and has at last given rise to the Système International (SI) which is accepted by most countries.

The actual processes of measurement, the techniques for comparing with standards, are purely physical. But because the comparisons are given numerical form, any further manipulation with the measures involves arithmetic. To pace out two sections of fence to measure them is a physical activity; to find the total length from this data calls for the number skills of addition.

Measure at primary level has a very important function outside the range of its physical applications, in that it can first present the need for fractional parts and hence calls for an extension of the number system as originally devised for counting discrete objects. Since measurement consists in comparing physical quantities with units, such as length with metres, it does not follow that a mere count of metres set end to end is sufficient; 4m can be too long and 3m too short. From examples such as these, the pupil can see the need for 'parts' of a metre.

The need is met by extending the number system to include fractions. These, like all numbers, are abstract, and have rules for computation which need to be learnt. Nevertheless, the practical activity of measuring provides the experience from which vulgar or decimal fractions can be abstracted. What is more, it helps the pupil to understand why particular rules are necessary, so that the two skills of measurement and computation can develop side by side.

Where formal computation is not used in practice, there seems little justification for extensive work with it in class. Measures no longer call for special algorithms with mixed and very variable exchange values, so that a pupil's basic need is seen as general skill with pure number with a full realization of how the number processes apply to measures. The use of measure itself is a physical rather than a mathematical skill.

The accurate recording of measures is more important than computation with them, and each child could make and keep a 'measurement book' in which he tabulates his own vital statistics and any other results that he obtains. The data thus collected can be the source of other work later.

2 Measure and the stages in learning

The formulation by Jean Piaget of the three stages by which a child is held to arrive at his mature grasp of a concept seems to express very clearly the growth of an understanding of measure. For the purposes of this chapter the Piagetian stages will be followed, although this does not imply an uncritical acceptance of all the findings of Piaget and his numerous disciples. The measures in question are those whose measurement is regarded as part of the mathematics programme at first or middle school levels.

The three stages in learning and assimilating any concept can be taken, as far as measure is concerned, as

Stage One: Preconceptual

Here the child has been brought into contact with situations from which the concept can be abstracted, but so far has formed no quantitative concepts corresponding to measure.

Stage Two: Transitional

Here the concept has begun to be abstracted, and is grasped in relation to one or a limited number of simple situations.

Stage Three: Conceptual

Here the learner has fully abstracted the concept and is sure of its connotation in most relevant situations.

An example to illustrate these stages can be noted very briefly here; three typical situations involving the concept of area are given, one of which fits each stage.

First Activity – Stage One

A baby is confined to a play pen, and shows pleasure when the pen is removed to give him the run of the room.

Second Activity – Stage Two

An older child is given a standard carpet tile and is asked how many are needed to cover a given rectangular area.

Third Activity – Stage Three

As a result of work in biology the child realizes that the leaf of a plant functions by presenting as much surface area as possible to light and atmosphere. He is asked to estimate the total area presented by the leaves of a plant.

If the three stages are accepted as steps in learning measurement, a general scheme of working to satisfy them would be as follows:

1 Preliminary activities to put the child in situations from which the concepts can be developed.

2 An introduction to measurement, with activities that lead to formulation of the concepts.

3 Measurement to given degrees of accuracy, with practice in estimation.

4 Activities involving computation with measures, as far as possible linked with daily use.

5 Discussion of measuring instruments and their calibration, and the choice of instruments for a given use.

6 Situations *not* designed specifically to bring in or practise measurement, but which make use of and hence reinforce the concepts.

The three stages are not hard and fast divisions, but it can be seen that **2–4** above fit in with the Transitional Stage, and that **5** and **6** imply that the pupil is at the Conceptual Stage.

Any actual scheme of work could usefully follow the steps given above, even though schemes are likely to vary considerably in detail and sequencing. It is necessary to expand these steps into possible approaches to each of the quantities normally included in the primary or lower school curriculum.

Of the basic measures, those of angle and temperature are conceptually less simple, and are not included in this chapter. The quantitative measure of speed, difficult to grasp since it is a ratio of two other measures, is also deferred.

3   Length, capacity, area and volume

The traditional sequence of length, area, volume goes back to Euclid's geometry. Liquid capacity usually appears as a separate topic. This treatment probably does not correspond to the development of the child's knowledge during the preconceptual stages, although it is followed in the development of the units used for measuring them. This has often resulted in imposing a formal sequence on teaching that does not keep pace with the understanding of the pupil, who may then never reach the full conceptual stage.

Convenience in writing this section results in an 'end-on' treatment of the topics, but in class one would expect to take only a few steps of one before beginning informal discussion of the other.

It would seem that a child's first experiences could be analysed in terms of capacity and volume; he can or cannot drink a proffered quantity of liquid, an object appears as big or small. Distance, one imagines, first appears in terms of the effort needed to reach something, or the tiredness induced by a walk.

In school, the child may be introduced to measure by being shown how to obtain the linear dimensions of a solid object by means of a rigid rule, so that he is beginning with an activity already well into the transitional stage. It cannot be assumed that the primary child is safely beyond the preconceptual stage, and one would recommend that early work should be informal activity from which the concepts of measure can be abstracted. A child who, rightly, feels that he is too old to play with water or building blocks, but who has not had a chance of doing these things when younger, is usually at a disadvantage when more abstract thinking is called for.

Measure is a topic that should be taken slowly, and needs extensive preliminary treatment, without formal units. Any separation of them into the traditional topics is probably unnecessary. Stringing beads together suggests the concept *length*, building towers of cubes suggests *height*, which is not at first seen as an equivalent to length. But the towers of cubes also suggest *volume*, and the suggestion is reinforced by repacking the cubes. Play with flat tiles, shapes or jigsaw puzzles relates to area, but so does pouring liquid from a bottle into a wide shallow dish.

Measurement of length

The success of any scheme of work lies in moving smoothly from these exploratory situations into the second stage of concept formation. The adjectives long, wide, deep and so on lead to the questions of how long, how wide, how much deeper, and the need for numerical statements emerges. At first, the pupil can work with any units chosen for convenience in any given situation – paces, spans, feet, cupfuls. Eventually the situations become more complex. Comparisons can be called for in positions separated in time or locality, and the need for a *standard* unit is seen.

At this point the appropriate standard unit is presented and its use demonstrated or discussed. No child can 'discover' the metre; at some stage the teacher has to ensure that the measures are available and that his pupils are aware of them. Length and capacity can emerge side by side, but from now on the formal development of area and volume must wait because they are measured in derived units and have been made to depend on length.

In spite of the apparent convenience of measuring small objects, one recommends that early work is done with individual metre rods and then perhaps a trundle wheel. The distance along corridors and across playgrounds is more directly related to the early ideas of distance than that between the edges of a desk top, and, moreover, works with the agreed unit, the metre, chosen for its general utility. The sub-divisions half and quarter metres are possible.

"Our classroom is $15\frac{1}{2}$ metres long" is a permissible usage, common in the metricated countries.

Most children need to be shown a technique for using a measuring rod, or at least helped to develop one by a series of leading questions. Young children will cheerfully pick up and put down a metre rod without noticing gaps, overlap or departures from a straight line. They need to learn to mark out a line or stretch a string if there is no obvious trace, and to mark the position of the end of the rod or grasp the dodge of using two rods put down alternately. They also need to keep systematic records of their measurements; in this as in other topics, careful tabulation of results keeps the school activity in line with actual use in the adult world.

Measuring smaller objects is not merely a matter of replacing the metre with the centimetre; the actual technique is different because the unit is not used as a 'pace', but sub-divides a longer rule. The centimetre is introduced as a convenient small unit, chosen so that

100 cm = 1 m.

One would suggest a rule marked in centimetres only. Most children would need to be shown how to bring the zero on the rule into line with the beginning of the object or interval measured, although for younger children an unnumbered scale with coloured intervals which need to be counted might be advisable. Children could even make a calibrated rule for themselves by pasting a strip of centimetre graph paper to a stout card.

The activity can be simplified and controlled by providing for measurement a number of strips of card, coloured or marked for reference, cut to exact known lengths and recorded by the teacher. Once a pupil has measured these correctly, he can pass on to less contrived objects. Classroom collections of containers and packages can be used; most of them will be within a convenient range of size. At this stage, the new concept of measurement to the nearest unit arises, and needs to be discussed.

A line may be more than 7 cm long but less than 8 cm. The pupil will probably need to be shown the technique to estimate by eye whether the line finishes nearer the 7 or the 8 marked on the rule. If the line appears to end exactly half way between the 7 and the 8, there is now a convention to be stated; always go to the unit above. The pupil would thus measure a box whose width is 75 mm as 8 cm to the nearest centimetre.

The diagram illustrates the three cases.

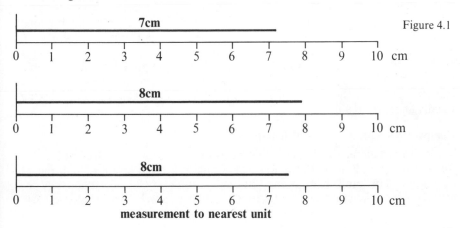

Figure 4.1

Once the pupil has begun to measure objects, that is, to associate with them a number read off from a measuring instrument, he could also begin to estimate, to associate the number by eye. This is something we do in everyday life more often than measuring.

The routine 'estimate, measure, record' could become the accepted form of measurement in class. The keeping of a book of measurements is not only worthwhile in itself, but provides sets of results which can be the data for other exercises. A book can be kept in this form:

Measure	Guessed	Measured	Error
Length of classroom	15 m	$18\frac{1}{2}$ m	$-3\frac{1}{2}$ m
New pencil	16 cm	14 cm	$+2$ cm
Edge of desk	60 cm	71 cm	-11 cm

The notation in the last column is a natural one. The guess has either added to or subtracted from the measure, and so one writes $+$ if the guess is high and $-$ if low. Later, the notation will link up with directed numbers, but at this stage is suggested to the pupil for convenience only.

The subdivision of the centimetre into millimetres should not be hurried; certainly pupils should be used to working accurately to the nearest centimetre for some time before being expected to measure in these rather small units, chosen for their technical convenience rather than their suitability for young eyes and fingers. The engineering convention that all detail measurement should be in millimetres only is not suitable for the younger child. Older pupils could be given measurement sheets having accurately measured lines in cm and mm ruled on them for practice, but indeed many adults are not used to such fine measures.

Parallel with this measurement practice as described should come work with flexible or curved lines. The question can be asked, "How long is this skein of wool or this ball of string?" Discussion will suggest that what is wanted is to stretch it out into a straight line, and this at once leads to lengths and distances measured on curved objects – definitely Stage Three topics in the child's development.

Measurement of an irregular line such as a route on a road map, by dividing it into short intervals each taken as straight, takes the concept even further, and is the principle of the map-measuring wheel.

The pupil will also need to meet, quite early on, the multiple unit for long distances, the kilometre. It would be possible for children to perambulate a playground till they had 1000 clicks on a trundle wheel, but they are likely to get more fun than instruction from the activity. A better approach would probably be to list the distances of familiar places starting from the school, with the teacher – and later the class, when scale and the use of maps is familiar – taking the distances from a map.

Computation with measures of length

The point has already been made that measures are for use and are not excuses for computation. Practical situations when lengths need to be added, subtracted or multiplied by numbers do occur, but not often in everyday life. When they do, actual commercial practice in so far as it affects the householder usually restricts the computation to measures taken to the nearest unit or half unit – timber and the like is sold in multiples of ready-cut lengths. The precise calculations of the quantity surveyor are no part of the education of the schoolchild.

Nevertheless, linear measures can be combined by the rules of arithmetic, although the processes are actually applied to the *numbers* that record the measures. 3 m+2 m=5 m arises for two logically independent reasons; because 3+2=5 and because lengths are physically additive. Computation with integral measures of length is simply a matter of inserting the unit symbols into standard algorithms.

As with money, computation if it is needed does not depend on a full grasp of the decimal notation. If 1 m=100 cm, any length can be recorded in metres and centimetres using the point merely as a separator, exactly as for £p. One would emphasize that the commercial and technical recommendations avoid the use of decimal points entirely by expressing all measures in the smallest unit thus

$$1 \cdot 37 \text{ m} = 137 \text{ cm} \qquad 1 \cdot 462 \text{ m} = 1462 \text{ mm}.$$

Subdivisions of a millimetre would only occur in precision engineering or scientific work. There seems to be no good reason why schools should not follow the recommendations for avoiding decimals with older children. To do so adapts the same conventions in the classroom as outside it, and not to do so introduces gratuitous difficulties. All computation then reduces to operations with integers, and follows exactly the processes already being learnt.

Liquid capacity

So far the topic of measure has been developed using units of length, without reference to other measures. This has been done for convenience in presentation and is not intended to suggest a similar order in the classroom. Some formal approach to liquid capacity could well, if the teacher prefers, come before the first steps in linear measure. It is a relatively simple topic at primary level because great accuracy is not called for.

The preliminary activity suggested is to compare the capacities of containers of various shapes – modern packaging provides a wide range of bottles and jars, often very deceptive in containing less than their sizes would suggest – either by direct transfer from one to another or by using a given small container as a measure. As before, the need to discuss results soon calls for a standard unit, and so the litre is presented. There are now, as well as measuring vessels, many bottles on the market which hold 1 litre (including those marked, in Imperial measures, 35 fluid ounces).

Using the standard measure, the capacity of buckets, bowls and sinks can be recorded. The half litre is a useful measure, and a pair can easily be contrived by sharing the contents of a litre plastic bottle equally with an empty one, marking the two levels and cutting them off with a fine hacksaw just above the marks. The subdivision of the litre can be discussed soon after the subdivision of the metre. Here the sub-unit is the millilitre (ml) where

$$1 \text{ l} = 1000 \text{ ml}.$$

This is rather small for primary use, but the pupil's number knowledge should now be able to cope with

$$\frac{1}{2} \text{ l} = 500 \text{ ml}$$
$$\frac{1}{4} \text{ l} = 250 \text{ ml}.$$

The standard medicine spoon gives a measure of 5 ml, which provides familiarity with smaller quantities of liquid.

Wide ranges of calibrated measures are obtainable for laboratory use, but most of these are not suitable for the primary age range. As with all measuring apparatus, one must not equate the precision of calibration with the skill of the user. Children can easily use a measuring cylinder by pouring in water and reading the graduations, but one should not puzzle them by a discussion of meniscus errors and parallax! Accuracy to the nearest division is all that can be expected. For older primary pupils a few beakers in 50 ml, 100 ml and 150 ml sizes are essential – these are obtainable, as are measuring cylinders, in both glass and plastic. Very good sets of plastic measures are now manufactured. One would hope that from an early stage manipulating fluids and their containers would also be combined with exercises in weighing and balancing.

Any problem that arises as, for example, in finding the total quantity of coffee needed to supply a gathering of people, calls more for common sense than computation. Anyone who had to make this coffee, if he could not draw on his own or someone else's experience, would probably fill cups with water from a jug to make a rough count and then multiply up to get a number safely above the expected attendance. He certainly would not measure the capacity of the cup and multiply by this figure.

Area

The general concept of area or surface is not quantitative. One readily sees that one carpet is bigger than another, or that a sponge has more exposed surface than a ball of the same size. The concept of a *measure* of area is more elusive. It is arrived at only with difficulty because equal areas can be enclosed by very different shapes and effectively occupy (or 'take up') different amounts of available space.

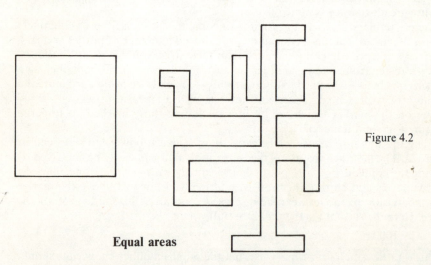

Figure 4.2

Equal areas

Many adults associate area with 'length times breadth', the residue of half-forgotten lessons on the area of rectangles. This is useful if one needs the area of rectangles, but may be a barrier to a more general concept.

Measure is always comparison with a standard, but with area the actual process of comparison is not obvious. It is very strongly recommended that early work with area should be with irregular shapes, with the rectangle arising as a very special case after the concept of area measurement is firmly grasped.

A possible move to take the child from his preconceptual stage is to ask which member of a group has the largest hand. Presumably this would be done by direct comparison. Later, perhaps as a direct outcome of a discussion on how plants 'breathe', one could ask which of two leaves presents the most surface to light and air, the one of smooth outline and the other deeply lobed. As a convenient step, one can trace the outline of leaf or hand on a sheet of paper. Then, from directed discussion, can come the technique of covering the area with suitable units, all of the same size and shape. The use of a unit such as a coin soon suggests the need for a shape that can cover the outline without gaps, and the transition into tiling operations, with standard tiles, can be made. Later the pupil will need to investigate in detail the possible shapes for a tiling unit, but at this stage the work is not intended to be systematic. Interesting material such as postage stamps or packet labels can be used.

If a few extra tiles are used and cut up to fill in the gaps at the edges of the outline, an approximate measure of the area is obtained, although this last step introduces a new factor; the possibility of subdividing the units in any desired way.

Discussion of the most convenient of the possible shapes for a standard unit and trials with triangles or other shapes leads to the suggestion of a square which can be linked to the unit of length by making its side 1 m or 1 cm. Thus the pupil is eventually presented with the metre squared (or square metre) and the smaller centimetre squared which he will use for most class purposes. An example of the square metre can be pinned up in the classroom. Note, however, that *any* uniform squares would be as convenient for actually covering an area; the square of side 1 m or 1 cm is chosen for numerical convenience in totalling the final result. Once the standard unit is decided, areas can be found much more conveniently by tracing the outline on squared paper and counting the squares. Not many children will at first see the need for a technique for dealing with the parts of squares.

Teachers will note that in work on area the child is asked to accept an entirely different use of the word 'square'. He will be quite familiar with the square as a shape, but in the phrase 'a square metre' shape is not referred to; it is merely an area equal to that of a metre square. For this reason, 'metre squared' and 'centimetre squared' are probably better, although they are less frequently found at present.

A basic exercise is to divide a unit square into parts by tearing, assembling the parts into an equivalent area of irregular shape, and labelling the results.

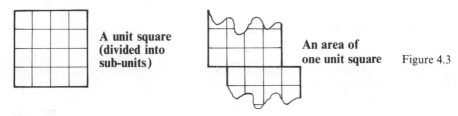

A unit square (divided into sub-units)

An area of one unit square   Figure 4.3

A child can paste examples in his notebook.

A failure in the development of the concept of area is sometimes shown by a confusion of area and perimeter, which are not seen to be independent. A useful exercise here is to construct, by shading in squares or parts of squares on a squared grid, polygonal shapes of constant area but changing perimeter.

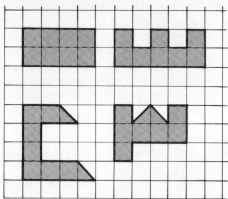

Figure 4.4

Equal areas – different perimeters

Another activity is to stretch out a large loop of thread into rectangles or other shapes which have different areas, although the perimeter remains unchanged. Children do not readily agree that the areas change. The key step in the child's grasp of the concept of area is not in being able to measure it, but in realizing that it is quite independent of shape. Any activity that helps this is worthwhile. The pupils may, for example, cut 25 squares of the same size from squared paper (2 cm grid is a useful size for this) and paste them down to make a set of '25-square men', all different. Children could also construct tangrams. A square of coloured gummed paper is marked out as shown in the diagram and cut into seven pieces.

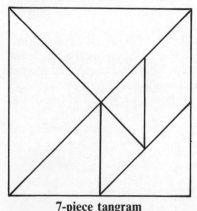

Figure 4.5

7-piece tangram

Children often show great ingenuity and a certain visual wit in arranging these pieces into pictures; as each is made it can be stuck on a classroom frieze whose caption notes that all the pictures are of the same area.

Treatment of the rectangle, it is suggested, should be delayed till the concept of area is firmly fixed. Although the pupil finds himself surrounded by rectangular objects – doors, windows, tables, tiles, bricks, courtyards and innumerable others, it is worth noting that the rectangle, apart from its occurrence as the face of certain crystals, is entirely an artifact. It is universal in the work of man; it is almost unknown in nature. A lively class might like to discuss why.

The rectangle is a very special case in that it is built up from the actual units of area, the square units, in a pattern that allows its area to be computed from its linear measurements. The pattern is clear from an example.

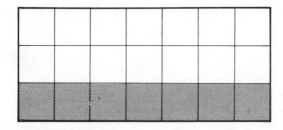

Figure 4.6

In the figure the rectangle is 7 cm long and 3 cm wide. Along one edge fits a row of 7 centimetre squares, whose total area is thus 7 cm². Since there are 3 such rows, multiplication gives

Area $= 3 \times 7$ cm²
$= 21$ cm².

Alternatively, one notes that there are 3 rows each of 7 units and then writes

Area $= (3 \times 7)$ cm²
$= 21$ cm².

The bracketed form makes it clear that the 21 is the product of two pure numbers, but the first form corresponds to 3 lots of 7 articles. A comment is needed on the frequently met form

Area $\doteqdot 3$ cm $\times 7$ cm
$= 21$ cm².

Strictly speaking, only numbers can be multiplied together. Centimetres cannot be multiplied by centimetres, any more than bricks by bricks. It is, however, a common convention to write the *dimensions* of a rectangle using $\times$ to read 'by' so that one has a rectangle 3 cm $\times$ 7 cm. This will be found in extensive use and must be accepted. If the product is known, then

Area of rectangle 3 cm $\times$ 7 cm $= 21$ cm²

becomes acceptable.

The point may appear pedantic, but a fully developed concept of area (as needed later if the pupil ever studies the calculus) has to grasp the distinction. For a rectangle, the computation reduces to finding the product of the number of units in the length and the number in the breadth. This gives the all too familiar

Area $=$ length $\times$ breadth

whose constant repetition has already been suggested, on page 68, as responsible for confused concepts later.

As far as possible, one would like computation to arise from practical situations. A set of accurately cut cardboard rectangles for measurement and computation of area seems to have more point than pages of examples. Truly practical examples involving area are more likely to be met at secondary level – in calculating total rainfall for instance. Carpets are priced by the metre square or other square unit, but, as with curtains and wallpaper, are fitted in terms of length of run and width. The coverage of paint is sometimes given in metres squared per litre, but this calls for only the roughest estimate of the area to be covered.

When the area of a rectangle is understood as a special case, the triangle can be discussed with abler children. By cutting a rectangle along the dotted lines as in the diagram

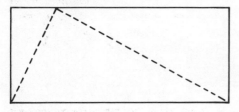

Figure 4.7

a pupil can be led to discover that the two pieces removed fit exactly over the triangle left, so that the area of the triangle is half that of the original rectangle. The next and essential step is to show that beginning with *any* triangle, one can extend it to a rectangle of the same base, so that the original height of the triangle becomes the breadth of the rectangle.

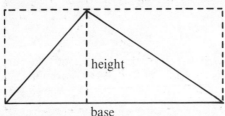

Figure 4.8

This step can only be taken if the pupil is fully aware of what is meant by the *height* of a triangle, which is not easy to see if the shape is orientated as in the diagram.

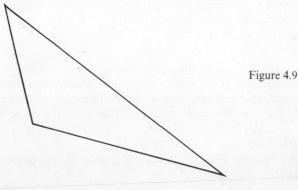

Figure 4.9

72

It should be clear that this exercise in area must await an adequate knowledge of plane shapes, and that older pupils suddenly faced with the formula

$$A = \tfrac{1}{2} bh$$

may well experience difficulties that an informal Stage Two treatment could avoid.

A formal treatment of the area of a circle is probably not advisable at primary level, although some attempt to look at the relationship between diameter and perimeter can be made informally.

Children could also investigate the relation between the areas of squares whose sides are increased by factors of 2, 3, 4 . . ., preferably by making them up with squared paper.

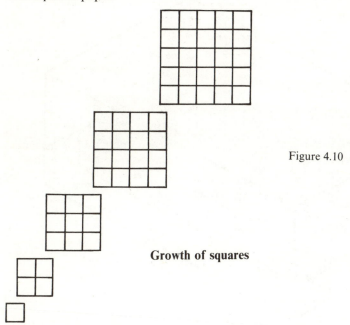

Figure 4.10

Growth of squares

The areas increase by the factors 4, 9, 16 . . ... These numbers are the squares of the terms in the first sequence.

Volume

One of a child's earliest experiences must be of cups or containers seen to be full or empty, so that the situations from which the concept of volume is later abstracted precede those of length. Nevertheless, the abstraction itself comes much later. The final recognition of volume and capacity as equivalent concepts taken in different contexts is a Stage Three process implying a confident grasp of both.

It is likely that the best approach to volume is to establish the link with capacity early on by displacement processes. This can be done quite simply by sinking large stones of various sizes in suitable containers of water and noting the rise in level. The stones which displace more have the bigger volume. From this

73

beginning, the experience gained with area should help the pupil to make a transition to the use of a formal unit of volume. At first, this is not connected with the displacement activities. Using centimetre cubes, supplied commercially, the pupil can build up shapes and count the cubes used. If the shape is a rectangular block, he will see that each layer is built of rows of unit cubes, so that for a block of length 7 cm, of width 4 cm and height 3 cm

$$\text{Volume} = 3 \times 4 \times 7 \text{ cm}^3$$
$$= 84 \text{ cm}^3$$

since the unit cube of side 1 cm can be said to have a volume of 1 cm³. Thus the centimetre cubed becomes the standard unit.

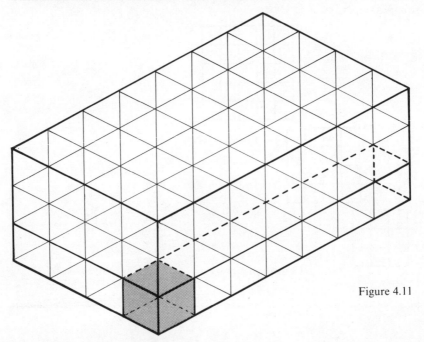

Figure 4.11

Block made with unit cubes

Shapes other than rectangular blocks can be built up with unit cubes, whose volumes are given by the cubes used.

The next step in refining the concept is difficult and should not be forced. The pupil has in fact made two disparate approaches to volume, by displacing a liquid and by analysing a very limited range of shapes into unit cubes with the rectangular block as a special case. For some children, it might be necessary to leave it at that.

For the older or more capable pupil, an approach to displacement volume can be made using a displacement can. This is, however, not an easy device to make or use satisfactorily, but for children able to cope with it it gives results with solids whose volume could not otherwise be found. A displacement can is made by punching a hole in the side of an empty tin with the top removed – the wheel type tin openers leave a smooth safe edge – and fixing in a short length of rubber tube slanting steeply downwards. Most waterproof glues and sealing compounds make a good joint. Filled with water, the level rapidly falls to that of the tube. If a lump of plasticine or putty is dropped in, the displaced water runs through the tube and can be caught in a separate container. The can does not work satisfactorily without the tube, or if the tube, is too narrow, because of surface tension effects.

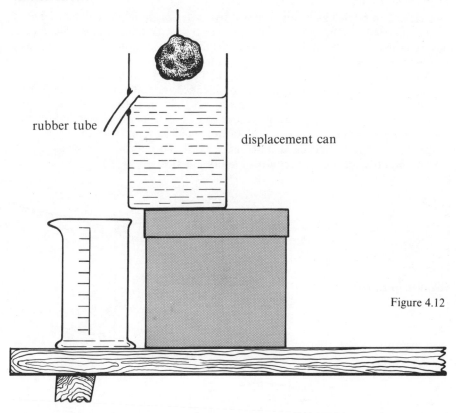

rubber tube

displacement can

Figure 4.12

If the outlet hole is at all greasy and the plasticine is put in very slowly, quite large lumps can be added without any run off at all! A few drops of detergent in the water help.

With this apparatus, the volumes of suitable solids such as stones, pieces of metal and the like can be compared. The teacher could tell the child that a given stone *displaces* so many millilitres of water; this introduces a useful technical word in a context where it can be understood. If the solid floats, the method cannot be used, and it is recommended that the matter should be left at that. The physics of flotation is too difficult to discuss at this stage.

The metric system has a direct connection between volume and capacity in that a litre is defined in terms of the metre cubed. One should note that the litre is one thousandth part of a metre cubed by definition and not by experiment. An open cubical box of thin card each of whose edges is 0·1 m (or 1 decimetre), carefully made and waterproofed with hot wax or several coats of polyurethane varnish, can be shown to hold a litre by filling it from a litre bottle, although the probable errors are large. A capable pupil could make such a box and demonstrate it to his classmates. They are also obtainable commercially made in sheet plastic.

Once the connections

$$1 \, \text{l} = 1000 \, \text{cm}^3$$
$$1 \, \text{ml} = 1 \, \text{cm}^3$$

are clear, the pupil has at his disposal two ways of finding a volume. Given a rectangular block, he can find its volume by measurement and calculation; given an irregular shape, he finds it by displacement, taking each millilitre as a centimetre cubed.

Any volumes expressed as formulae, such as are given for spheres, cylinders, pyramids and so on, should, it is recommended, be left till much later. Older pupils frequently learn such formulae without full conceptual understanding.

The investigation suggested for areas can be extended usefully to volumes, using unit cubes. The pupil can build a cube whose side is twice that of the unit cube, and will note that eight units are needed. To build a cube whose side is three times that of the unit requires 27 cubes, and so on.

Growth of cubes

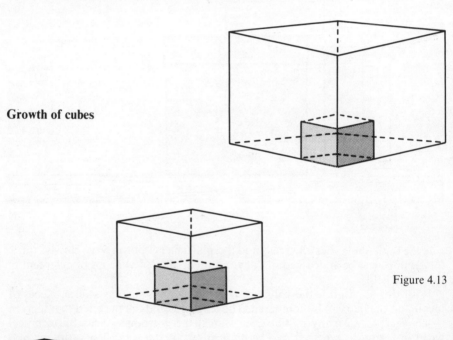

Figure 4.13

A diagram, as given, is not easy for the pupil to read since only the conventions of perspective enable it to be interpreted as a growing cube made up with smaller cubes, and the presence of many of these needs to be inferred rather than observed. If the exercise is to be done at all, actual cubes need to be used.

The full implications of the side/area/volume ratios of growing squares or cubes are too deep for children. This is one of those background activities whose meaning extends with general knowledge and maturity, and so is worth doing informally at primary level. The biology teacher is particularly interested in these relationships, since an organism has functions such as cooling which depend on surface area and others, such as the need for nutrients, which depend in part on its volume.

4 Money

In money matters, as in measurement, number skills impinge on everyday life. One can, by a loose analogy, think of money as a measure of value, although the units of currency do not behave as the normal units of other measures.

This is an important distinction. An actual metre rod can be thought of as 100 units each of which is a centimetre, but a £1 note is merely equal in value to 100 pence as an exchange. Moreover, a centimetre can be subdivided both physically and notionally, into ten parts, whereas 0·1p is purely notional and not represented by a coin. This implies that the decimal point has a different function in writing money, and can best be thought of as a separator between pounds and pence. Ordinary money calculations can be done without reference to decimal arithmetic as such, and our decimal currency is so called because it works with an exchange value of ten. The 'decimal point' is avoided as such in this section.

Teachers and parents will realize that the problems of money management are social or domestic rather than mathematical; the actual arithmetic of daily cash handling and shopping is a necessary skill, but is not very relevant to solving the financial problems of adult life. It is money sense rather than number skills that matters. The National Savings Committee publish money booklets aimed at a programme of education in money sense, and these are supplied free to schools on application.

Most children learn to handle money in small amounts before they begin school, and to be able to do so is comparable with learning to speak rather than learning to read. Certainly, older children, who may be backward and unable to cope with computation, have no difficulty in actually handling money; if in later life their families fail to cope with money problems, it is more than number skills that are lacking.

The three stages in the child's development of money sense are, approximately:

Stage One   Handling and recognition of coins, with growing awareness that coins are exchangeable for goods.

Stage Two   Knowledge of exchange values. Numerical equivalence between currency and prices. The Four Rules in so far as they have practical application. Efficient handling of cash in shopping situations.

Stage Three The notional handling of money as distinct from receiving and spending coins. Money as a measure of value or worth. The fiduciary aspect of money in savings accounts, investments, banking and so on.

Normally the work of a primary school would not go much beyond the second stage; although most children learn to think of money as value and to appreciate savings.

School work in Stage One would be completed in the infant school, where teachers could check that their pupils can recognize coins and have experience in surrendering them for goods in shopping situations. The child also begins to record money in writing and to read prices.

At this point the structure of the decimal currency becomes important and needs to be considered. The word 'decimal', with its suggestions of difficult computation, was responsible for many of the misgivings felt by older people before the new currency appeared in 1971. All that it means in context is that an exchange value in tens replaces the former 12/20 exchanges in passing from pence to pounds.

It is strongly recommended that in teaching it should merely be stated that the penny is a sub-unit of the pound; that 100p are equal in value to £1, and that sums involving both pence and pounds are written with a point which acts as a *separator* between the two. Indeed, the banks have replaced the point with a dash for sums written on cheques. The 'decimal point' need not be mentioned. In any computation the columns of pounds and pence are handled separately, with the carry over that arises if the pence columns total 100 and more.

In detail, this suggests that prices can be analysed in terms of the basic tokens of £1, 10p and 1p, as in the table of prices of £3·39, 7p, £1·40, £2·99.

£1 notes	· ·	10p coins	1p coins
3	·	3	9
0	·	0	7
1	·	4	0
2	·	9	9

This now corresponds to the standard fully recorded form of a sum of money. For convenience, of course, it is better to write 7p rather than £0·07, and this is the accepted convention. If quantities are being entered in columns, though, the full form is important. One would write

£
3·39
0·07
1·40
2·99

and it would be unwise to permit any contraction at school levels.

Cash register printouts, which most children meet before they begin 'money sums' in school, usually print extra zeros in the tens and hundreds column, often in small type.

If children cannot be given real coins to handle, they can at least work with realistic tokens in 'shopping play' exercises. A useful activity is to make up a given sum in as many different ways as possible from a given number of coins. Another is to list articles that can be bought for 1p, 2p, 5p, 10p . . . stopping at a figure realistic for a child's likely experience.

The activities and any recording that accompanies them are easily justified – but it is a fact that, outside school and in a number of specialist occupations, people do not often compute with money. Given the column analysis of page 78 the algorithms for addition and multiplication follow those of Chapter 2. The difficulty is in practising them with calculations that are not just mechanical arithmetic. A few sets of sums, products and differences can be done to maintain skills, and the suggestion is repeated that these should not be done as 'decimal' calculations, so described, but as £p computation with the point as separator.

More useful in keeping the work at a level within the bounds of buying and spending are sums to which the pupil is asked to give a 'story'. This extends practice both in recording and in vocabulary.

Example

```
    p
   26
 +  7
 ────
   33
 ────
```

Story

I spent 26p on a new painting book and 7p on a paintbrush, so I spent 33p in all.

Done neatly with thought given to the reasonableness of the story, each exercise takes time so that only a few can be finished, yet a few sums done in this way are probably of more value than pages of mechanical work.

In any case, the decimal currency now means that the separate algorithms for handling the exchange values of £ s d have vanished, and money calculations are absorbed into general number work. Apart from the suggested technique for dealing with the separator, money problems become more a matter of social than numerical training.

If needed, the extended algorithms go as before. For example, if one needed the cost of 7 railway tickets at £1·62, the computation could be, if uncontracted

```
      £
    1·62
 ×     7             £
   ─────
    0·14      7 × 0·02
    4·20      7 × 0·60
    7·00      7 × 1·00
   ─────
   11·34
   ─────
```

It is, however, worth noting that the problem can be worked entirely in pence, since the cost of each ticket is 162p and hence the cost of 7 is (7×162)p. Since 100p=£1, the final cost of 1134p is written £11·34. The technique here is to remove the separator and replace it at the end of the calculation. It could be that a child having difficulty will find this method easier.

It is hard to justify any algorithm for the subtraction of money other than the physical complementary addition using coins that all shopkeepers use if they handle money at all. It is the one children will have to use if ever they work in a shop and need to give change. In actual situations difficulties are avoided. If one proffers 50p, for a purchase of $12\frac{1}{2}$p, the shopkeeper frequently begins by asking for the odd halfpenny, and then builds up, with coins, from 12p to 50p. The occasional sum with its 'story' seems to be all that is needed.

One should also remember that three-quarters of all shopping, item for item, is done under supermarket or self-service conditions. The tendency here is for automatic print-out bills, which compute and record the total purchase, the amount proffered and the change due. Many check-out machines issue the change as well.

Much of the original motive has gone from computational work with money, but this, of course, implies that extra effort must be made to get children to perform accurate reckoning in the few situations that call for it. Money sense rather than number skill is the need that remains for coping with finance in everyday life.

5 Time

Although we are all aware of the passage of time, the story of its measurement shows how difficult are the concepts involved. The child has to come to terms very early in life with clocks, which are quite modern compared with measuring rods and standard masses. He learns to associate bedtime with a certain position of the clock hands, and will probably recognize this long before a measured passage of time can have meaning for him.

As an instrument of measure, the clock is very complicated. No other familiar instrument gives its information with the aid of two separate pointers moving at different speeds, with the long one giving different readings from the short. There are also linguistic difficulties. The same time can be announced as 'two thirty-five', 'twenty-five to three' or 'fourteen thirty-five'. The difficulties many adults have had to adjust themselves to the 24-hour system might make them aware of the child's problems.

There are two distinct aspects of time measurement, whose relationship is not conceptually clear. The first is the measurement of an interval of time, the elapsed time, as measured by a stop-watch that always begins to record from zero. The other is the civil or calendar time, that fixes events by time and date. There is no reason why children should not meet minutes and seconds of elapsed time before they are confident of telling the time by clock; the words minute and second can be introduced in informal discussion and demonstrated. A thread

1 m long, with a bob of metal or clay, hung up as a pendulum swings seconds fairly closely, so that children can count as it swings. The minute can be appreciated as a minute's silence, timed by a watch, and then the stop-clock – a bench type with a large sweep seconds hand – can be introduced. The children can then hear and watch the seconds building up into minutes, and can be set to time various activities informally. This can be done before they are capable of recording the results; the activities are intended to make them familiar with the units of time measurement. One does not need to be able to tell the time to read a stop-clock.

With this experience behind them, children should learn to read a clock more easily. A large clock face with movable hands is in most infant and primary schools, and most teachers have their own preferred sequences for teaching. A familiar sequence is

hours
hours and half-hours (read as 'half past . . .')
hours and quarters (read as 'quarter past . . .')
hours and three-quarters (read as 'quarter to . . .').

In moving the hands from the hour to the quarter past, it is essential that *both* are moved. The minute-hand should, one feels, *never* be moved without reference to the movement of the hour-hand. Even if the adjustment is less than five minutes, the child should always be made aware that the hour-hand does in fact move. Many older children, asked to state the angle between the hands of a clock at half past six, will say it is zero.

Language and usage are real difficulties. Whatever is taught, the child will probably hear people say, 'minutes past . . .' to half past, and 'minutes to . . .' up to the hour, possibly with 'five and twenty' instead of 'twenty-five'. He will also hear such notations as 'three fifteen', 'three forty'. Telling the time is difficult because it is *not* mathematical; it is governed by idiomatic forms that are unlikely to be standardized.

If one had to recommend a teaching sequence that follows what appears to be the commonest usage, it would continue from above by counting in fives as

five past . . .
ten past . . .
till
twenty-five past . . .

and then *backwards* from

five to . . .
ten to . . .
till
twenty-five to . . .

Clearly local usage, the teacher's own preferences, or a school decision may modify this.

What is important is that the 24-hour system should be introduced as early as possible. It is now the national standard for all rail, bus, air and steamer time-tables, and children can scarcely avoid it. From the teaching point of view, it has the advantages of a fixed notation, although even here the spoken form adopts a convention that originated in the services and does not agree with the exchange value between hours and minutes.

In this notation, the hours run 00, 01, 02 . . . 10, 11 . . . 23, beginning at midnight, the minutes from 01 to 59. The minutes are separated from the hours either by a point or a space, although service usage often runs them together. Thus

    3.15 p.m. = 15.15 (said as fifteen fifteen)
    3.15 a.m. = 03.15 (said as 03 fifteen)
      6 a.m. = 06.00
      6 p.m. = 18.00

In speech the last two would be said as 06 hundred and 18 hundred. This service convention is probably here to stay. The classroom needs sets of timetables and, more useful by far since they are simpler, leaflets for bus or train special excursion offers. These, giving departure and arrival times, can be used to answer questions about the length of journeys.

The classroom will also need a model of the digital clock, now becoming increasingly common in railway and bus stations. With help, children can make their own from a strip of stout card cut with four sets of parallel slots as in the diagram.

Figure 4.14

Into these slots fit strips of paper whose ends can be joined to form loops. These carry the required digits and can be adjusted in the slots to display any required time. A more convenient form for classroom use is made with a cardboard box.

One would hope that the bold action taken by schools in adopting SI metric units would also extend to the use of the 24-hour clock and that school timetables should now follow the example of the transport undertakings. As with all measures, or indeed with usage in almost any situation, what is taught to the child, tends to persist in the adult. Many adults have difficulty with timetables because they have had to learn the 24-hour system late in life, but no child should find it anything but a simplification. It would certainly make learning to read the time more simple, if (but only if) the digital clock replaced the 12-hour dial in schools.

As the child learns to tell the time, the earlier informal work in elapsed time can be extended. This extension needs a cautious approach: it is very easy to take the physical activities to a point beyond the conceptual grasp of the children. The concept of elapsed time passes over into many higher order concepts involving rates of change, growth and decay, which are not easy to organize into a comprehensive understanding. Yet these activities, extended to observation and recording, can form a foundation for later work, and there is a wide range available for primary treatment.

Examples

Pendulum studies – time for 20 swings, effect of changes in length or in mass of bob, adjustment to beat seconds, shadow stick – lengths of shadows recorded at intervals.

Flow of liquids – flow from a perforated tin in equal intervals of time.

Activity timing – walking round the playground, running and swimming, completion of written tasks.

Many of these are suitable for making up into work cards, and some of them will be preliminary to work with speed, a more difficult concept involving both time and distance.

6   Mass and weight

Until recently, the word 'weight' did duty for both weight and mass in all but scientific usage. The phenomenon of weightlessness in satellite orbits is now well known, and enables an informal distinction to be made. It also enforces a decision on the use of the words in the classroom.

Weight, as a measure, is the gravitational pull on a quantity of matter. It extends quantitatively the preconceptual experience of exerting oneself to lift heavier or lighter objects. It varies slightly from place to place on the earth's surface, drops to about one sixth of its value on the surface of the moon, and vanishes altogether in a satellite in stable orbit. It is measured directly by the extension produced on a spring balance against the pull of the spring. Mass measures the quantity of matter subject to whatever gravitational pull there is, and does not change as weight changes. Mass can be experienced by trying to move a heavily laden canal barge a metre or so on a windless day, and then stopping the movement thus imparted. In this situation the weight of the barge is taken by the upthrust of the water; the muscular effort is directed at altering the motion of the mass.

A spring balance measures weight directly; a pair of scales balances masses by balancing their weights. The distinction is important. A spring balance would read low on the moon, but a pair of scales could be used normally, since both the object and the standard masses lose weight equally.

Nevertheless, the verb 'to weigh' has always been associated with any type of scale or balance, although these are almost always used to measure a quantity of substance and hence a mass. For this reason, in this book the words *mass* and *weight* follow the current scientific usage, but the actual operation of scales or balances is called *weighing*. This usage is recommended in schools. The preconceptual stages in weighing begin in very early infancy as the child lifts and handles objects and begins to use words such as light, heavy and their comparatives. The transitional stages are less easily arrived at and children need directed activity before formal measurement of mass is begun. This is partly because of the difficulty of separating the concept of mass from the more obvious characteristic of size or volume. Indeed, the muscles play tricks here, and tend to experience a large object as lighter than a small object having the same mass. It is easy to arrange strips in order of length or boxes in order of volume, but not easy to arrange objects in order of mass if they are made of very light or heavy materials, when the volumes are also very different.

On the other hand, a pair of scales does this very easily without standard masses – objects merely have to be balanced against one another. Solid objects and liquids can be compared by pouring water into an empty container till it balances a solid mass, and sand or beans can be weighed one against the other or against different objects.

The standard unit of mass, the kilogram, was chosen because of its convenience in the larger scale operations of commerce or industry. It is rather heavy, both for small children to handle and for classroom supplies and equipment. The gram, on the other hand, well adapted for the finer work of the science laboratory, is too small as a mass and if made of metal is easily lost. Masses in light high impact plastic are available, in multiples of 10 g, and these would seem ideal for the classroom. Centimetre cubes are also available in quantity, each of which is nominally 1 g. Between them, these plastic products meet most of the needs of classroom weighing. They are not very accurate, but are probably within the child's own limits of operation. Use of these masses allows the child to move from the initial concept of balancing to the operational concept of balancing against standards. He can also reproduce the standards using bags of sand or peas. The kilogram itself can be introduced informally, and used to weigh out kilograms of sand, stones, potatoes and the like.

The spring or lever balance with a straight scale or pointer moving round a dial is best introduced after the pupil is quite familiar with weighing by balancing. The usual domestic type with a single removable pan is, of course, the more convenient apparatus in the kitchen, but its use bypasses the fundamental balancing operation between masses. For this reason, it could be at first withheld from the classroom until children can weigh confidently with balance scales. Because it is the apparatus they might see at home the pointer type should certainly be introduced, but only after the concept of balancing weights is firmly established.

Pupils will probably find the kilogram most useful in measuring themselves. A set of bathroom scales can be bought cheaply. They usually have both metric and Imperial calibrations.

It would seem that any calculation that could arise with mass at this level would involve integers only. One might, for example consider the total weight of a school party's luggage in readiness for an air trip, where each item is weighed to the nearest kilogram, or try to extend a cookery recipe for four people to twenty, where quantities are usually rounded off to nothing finer than 10 g.

A group can also set out to estimate the mass of a wall by weighing a brick, making an allowance for mortar and then counting the bricks in a course and the number of courses.

A primary pupil is unlikely to approach a fully conceptual understanding of mass, which would include the clear distinction between mass and weight and the second-order concept of density which is the ratio between mass and volume. He should, however, be able to handle the concept operationally within the limits of his experience, and be presented with situations that extend this experience.

An apparatus of the sort used to illustrate the principle of moments gives a range of extended experience, although the children would not be ready for a formal discussion. It is available commercially, but can easily be made in the classroom.

The apparatus, although useful, should be treated informally. If, for example, one hangs 2 washers on a hook at a distance of 6 units, they will balance 3 washers at a distance of 4 and $2 \times 6 = 3 \times 4$. The apparatus is then only demonstrating that its operation follows the numerical rules for products; it provides a motive for recording products and an illustration of product relationships. It is not recommended for any other use. It certainly does not prove product relationships such as commutativity, although it displays them very effectively.

At a later stage, the device can be used in discussing the moments of forces and the laws of the lever, but this work is not appropriate, at least in any formal sense, to the primary classroom. The limit to any work is set by the understanding shown by the children.

7   The metric system and SI units

The metric system is one of the few enduring results of the French Revolution. In its original form and development, it had become rather clumsy, and it has now been modified by international agreement to a system of measures that meets the needs of measurement at all levels. This is the Système International or SI, which can be anglicized as Standard International.

The needs of the primary pupil within this system are so modest that they can be given here in full.

Basic units

There are seven fundamental units in SI and a few 'customary' units, whose use will soon be apparent. Of the seven, only four will appear in first or middle school courses of mathematics. These are

   The unit of mass – the kilogram (kg)
   The unit of length – the metre (m)
   The unit of time – the second (s)
   The unit of temperature – the Kelvin (K)

Of these, the Kelvin is for scientific purposes and will be replaced in ordinary use by the degree Celsius (°C). Officially, the word 'centigrade' is not used, because on the Continent it measures an angle, not a temperature, and confusion could result. The official second is extended by the *customary units*, year, month, week, day, hour, minute, so that the measurement of time remains unaltered.

Sub-units

To meet the need for smaller or larger units, multiples or submultiples of the basic units are given by prefixes as follows.

$$1\ 000\ 000 \text{ units} \quad \text{mega} - \text{(M)}$$
$$1000 \text{ units} \quad \text{kilo} \quad - \text{(k)}$$
$$\tfrac{1}{1000} \text{ unit} \quad \text{milli} \ - \text{(m)}$$

Thus for length, one has

1 kilometre (km) = 1000 metres (m)
1 metre (m)   = 1000 millimetres (mm)

In addition to these, the system allows, and indeed recommends for educational use, the submultiple *centimetre* (cm) where 1 m = 100 cm. There is also a named unit, the decimetre (dm), for one tenth of a metre, so that

1 m = 10 dm

This is rarely used and in its place, metres and tenths expressed in the decimal notation can be given. No other measures of length are called for in any situation likely to be met in school.

The original metric unit of mass was the gram (g) but, because this is rather small, the SI unit is the kilogram (kg) where

1 kg = 1000 g, as before.

The smaller unit is the milligram (mg).

1 g = 1000 mg

Since the kilogram itself is too small for goods in bulk, the megagram (Mg) is useful.

1 Mg = 1000 kg
     = 1 000 000 g

This is often called a metric tonne, and is within a few kilograms of the old Imperial ton.

Derived units

Area and volume

The measures for area and volume are derived from the unit for length in a familiar way. The unit of area is the metre squared (or square metre), written m^2, and this notation also applies to the multiples and submultiples km^2, cm^2, mm^2. For convenience, there is a 'customary unit' adopted from the original metric system. This is the hectare (ha).

1 hectare = 10 000 m^2

This unit is used for land measure, where the km^2 is too big and the m^2 too small. It is about the size of a standard football pitch.

Volume is measured using the cubic metre (metre cubed). There are the corresponding symbols m^3, km^3, cm^3, and mm^3. 1 m^3 of water has a mass of 1 metric tonne.

Liquid measure

Since liquids have traditionally been measured in special units, the system retains as a customary unit the litre (l) and its submultiple, the millilitre (ml).

1000 litres = 1 m^3

A litre of water can be taken as having a mass of 1 kilogram.

The entire range of measures needed for all purposes, not only in school, but for all other uses not specifically scientific or technical, can now be summarized (in descending order of size)

Mass	Mg, kg, g, mg
Length	km, m, cm, mm
Area	km^2, ha, m^2, cm^2, mm^2
Volume	m^3, cm^3, mm^3
Capacity	l, ml
Time	years, months, weeks, days, hours, minutes, seconds
Temperature	°C

The system also includes the customary unit for measuring angles, the degree (°) where

360° = 1 complete turn.

No other measures need be taught and no others are used within the system except for needs that only specialists will meet. If the above are properly learnt, the topic of measurement is complete, although the primary pupil is unlikely to achieve a mature standard of accuracy in applying his knowledge.

Where formal computation is not used in practice, there seems little justification for extensive work with it in class. Measures no longer call for special algorithms with mixed and very variable exchange values, so that a pupil's basic need is seen as general skill with pure number with a full realization of how the number processes apply to measures. The use of measure itself is a physical rather than a mathematical skill.

The accurate recording of measures is more important than computation with them, and each child could make and keep a 'measurement book' in which he tabulates his own vital statistics and any other results that he obtains. The data thus collected can be the source of other work later.

Chapter 5

SHAPE

1 Introduction

One of the most important changes in the content of mathematics in the primary school is that which gives a proper place to the study of elementary ideas of geometry. To many adults 'geometry' means the study of the theorems of Euclid which they themselves met at school. This is not a suitable approach for young children and is why this chapter is headed 'Shape' rather than 'Geometry'. Any geometry of the formal deductive type, that has been so common in secondary schools in the past, is obviously unsuitable for primary children. On the other hand, if we neglect a study of the ideas of shape and size, we are neglecting to study that aspect of the environment that is probably most familiar to the child. All those things which a child sees and uses every day have shape and size, and each child has a fund of experience which can be used in the exploration of the properties of these shapes.

One reason why the study of space and shape at the primary level is so important is that it introduces, in a very simple way, many of the ideas that one can call mathematical. To be able to name various shapes one has to classify them – to make a decision about what is to be called the 'same' and what 'different'.

For instance, in classifying certain shapes as squares one considers the corners, and the lengths of the sides, which fix the shape, but the size is irrelevant. All figures that are the shape of a square are called squares whatever their size. To classify shapes as triangles one looks at only one property, the number of sides or angles. Two triangles need be neither the same shape nor the same size. All those triangles which are the same shape but a different size are called *similar*; all those triangles which are the same shape *and* the same size are *congruent*.

The realization that these decisions as to 'same' and 'different' are being made and the understanding of what criteria are being used is of great importance. One of the activities that occurs most regularly in all mathematics is deciding what things are the same and what things are different.

This may seem a very sophisticated reason for introducing the ideas of elementary geometry into the primary school, but it is necessary to make it quite clear that the mere learning of the names of a number of different shapes is not in itself of any great value. It is the handling of shapes and the exploration of space in such a way that the children make decisions about how they will classify and describe what they are doing, because *they have seen that there is a need to have such a classification*, that make these ideas important for primary children.

2 Basic concepts of geometry

The basic elements of a study of shape and space that concern the mathematician are

> points
> lines (straight and curved)
> surfaces (flat and curved).

With these basic elements new elements can be made such as

> angles
> plane configurations
> solids.

Then various measurements can be made to describe

position	shape	regularity	congruence
size	symmetry	similarity	

If one were building an abstract mathematical structure, a beginning could be made by defining all these terms in roughly the order which is given here. The child, however, does not do this. He starts with the real world and the very young child's world is three-dimensional. He starts with solid shapes, and it is some time before he will think in terms of two dimensions. It is even longer before he is ready for such ideas as definitions of a point or line.

The brief notes that follow are to give an idea of the kinds of activities associated with the concepts listed at the beginning of this section that are suitable for young children.

Line – the idea of a line grows intuitively and with a young child there is probably no need to discuss what a line is. It is important, however, to realize that there are different kinds of lines – curved, straight, twisted, and an exploration of these using a piece of thread or string is worth while. For instance, he can be asked, "Can you make a straight line from this?"

If 'this' is a piece of string, it can be rubbed with chalk, pulled tight at the ends and snapped on the blackboard or floor when it will leave a chalked straight line. (In both Latin and Greek the equivalent of 'straight line' means a stretched linen thread.)

Later on when lines are used for drawing diagrams, they are used in different ways which can be formally defined. Should confusion arise due to the different ways in which lines are used, it may be helpful to classify them as follows, but the definitions given here are not in general suitable for young children.

In some instances, the line can be extended in either direction as far as is desired. This is called a *line* and can be indicated by

In other cases, the line finishes at a point at one end but continues as far as desired at the other. This is called a *ray* and can be drawn as

In other cases, a line is drawn which is a definite length and this is called a *line segment* and drawn as

Using these definitions 'two lines crossing at a point' can be drawn as

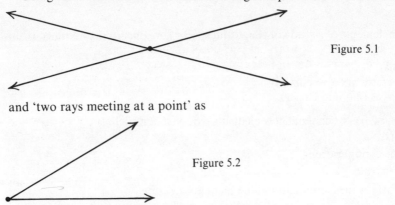

Figure 5.1

and 'two rays meeting at a point' as

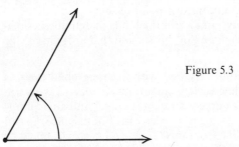

Figure 5.2

The arrows given here make a clear distinction, but are usually omitted in textbook diagrams.

Angle – the word angle gives difficulty because it is used in two different senses. It is said that a triangle has three angles (describing the corners) and it is also said that an equilateral triangle has an angle of 60° which is a measure of the amount of turn of one of the sides from the other, i.e.

Figure 5.3

This is a difficulty which can be overcome by using the word 'corner' to describe the angle of a figure in the early stages and by using the amount of turn as a measure of an angle.

Regular – regular rectilineal plane figures, i.e. in 2 dimensions, are ones in which all the angles are equal and all the sides are equal. Regular solids (3 dimensions) have all their edges and all angles equal. This means each face must be identical in shape and size, and also that the solid must look the same viewed from each corner (vertex).

Similar – similar figures (both 2 and 3 dimensions) are ones which are the same shape but a different size.

Congruent – congruent figures are figures which are the same shape and size. A plane figure can be superimposed exactly on another figure with which it is congruent. (This, in fact, is what the word 'congruence' means.)

Symmetry – the ideas of symmetry help children to classify and analyse shapes because the ideas are intuitive. Children know when things are symmetrical even before they know how to describe what this means.

3 Geometry of intuition

Children's first experiences will be of touch. They will handle solid objects like building bricks, boxes, cartons and packets. They will be learning to use words like straight, curved (of lines), flat, curved (of surfaces), round, short, long, etc. Any attempts to call things the 'same' or 'different' will be limited to ideas of size or very general shape. They will say that things are 'round' (balls, cylindrical tins) or 'square' (rectangular packets, bricks) but not make sharper distinctions.

The first ideas of classification come through counting corners, edges and faces of solids, and giving names to common shapes such as square, rectangle, circle and triangle.

There is a great deal of simple experience of this kind that has to be acquired over a long period of pre-school play at home and during the years in the infant school. The experience of handling and looking at shapes that a child meets in his daily life without any attempt to formalize the activity is essential to the work in the primary school. If the children have for some reason missed this experience, then it will be necessary for the teacher to provide this before starting on the work suggested for the primary stage, although he will spend far less time on it.

The first years in the primary school will be ones of exploration and discovery and the children will need apparatus that enables them to carry out these explorations. For shapes, the apparatus will be geo-boards, cut-out geometrical shapes, strips that can be joined by fasteners, squared paper and other kinds of grids, and boxes and containers of different shapes and sizes.

Most of the work on geo-boards that is suitable for young children can be done using only the 9 pin and 16 pin boards. There is much to be gained by using a piece of apparatus which enables the child to exhaust the possibilities of a situation. This is far easier to arrange with a small number of pins than it is on a board containing say 144 pins. For instance, it is possible to ask, "how many squares can you make on a 9 pin board?" since there are only 6 and most children would be able to find these. The number of squares that can be made on 144 pins is so great as to make it impracticable to ask a similar question.

A very important part of the work will be discussing with the children what they have done individually, in groups, and at times with the whole class. The teacher has a great deal of choice as to the order in which he introduces ideas to the children and the following account is intended only to give some help in the way they may be developed, and to show the benefit of using different kinds of shapes apparatus for exploring a topic. The division of activities into stages in what follows has only been done for convenience. There are, of course, no clear-cut stages but a gradual growth of ideas.

Stage I – The free exploration stage

The importance of this stage needs to be emphasized. It is of great value for children to be able to explore apparatus quite freely without work cards or other direction before being asked to undertake specific tasks.

At first, children will be given a geo-board and elastic bands and told to see what patterns they can make, or what compound shapes they can make with the cut-out shapes, or jointed rods. This enables them to explore the relationships between parts of the material and see what possibilities exist. In this 'free exploration' some children will make discoveries that will lead to more directed work later.

Stage II – First classification

If a child has been making patterns on a geo-board with elastic bands he will make a great many shapes. He can be asked what shapes are the 'same' and helped to choose some sort of classification. The following are a few of the many possibilities

Shapes with the same number of sides
Shapes with the same number of corners
Shapes made with the same number of pins (for geo-boards)
Shapes with the same area,

or, he could possibly choose a name that has been learnt previously, such as

square, rectangle, triangle, regular, symmetrical.

When this first classification has been chosen, it can be explored. A very effective way of giving direction to an exploration is the 'How many?' question. Examples are

How many different 3-sided shapes can be made on a 9 pin board?
How many different 4-sided shapes can be made on a 9 pin board?
How many different 3-sided shapes with the same area can be made on a 9 pin board?
How many different 4-sided shapes with just two equal sides can be made on a 9 pin board?

Similar questions can be asked of a 16 pin board, or of shapes with larger numbers of sides. Almost any classification of shapes can be phrased as a 'How many?' question.

Stage III – Development of a classification

Suppose that the first classification is of four-sided shapes, one could then ask if they are all squares, or rectangles, or what other four-sided shapes there are. Other questions that could be asked are

How many squares can you find on the 9 pin board?
Are all squares the same shape?
Are all the squares the same size?
What makes a shape square?

At this stage, either similar questions could be asked of all the 4-sided shapes, and then of those with other numbers of sides, or the square could be explored more thoroughly. It does not matter which is done, or if some other course is taken, the choice can safely be left to the children.

In order to show how work can proceed, take as an example the exploration of squares. It is helpful to use several different kinds of material, e.g.

Make squares with jointed strips.

Find as many square shapes as possible in the classroom, and one can ask

What can you say about the lengths of the jointed strips used to make a square?

Is the square frame made with the strips rigid?

If not, does it remain a square when the strips are moved?

This second question can lead to an interesting discussion. If the strip is moved so that the shape becomes

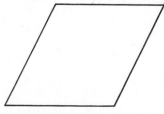

Figure 5.4

most children will say it is not a square; if the strips are moved carefully keeping the corners the same so that it takes up a position like this

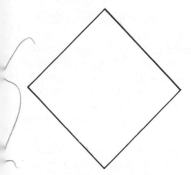

Figure 5.5

then many will still say it is not a square. Something is needed to check the corner and a folded right angle is the ideal instrument.

This now establishes that the square is a shape with all its sides equal and all its corners right angles, and the collection of shapes can be examined to see how many of those that are usually called 'square' are square when actually measured – there are some surprises in store!

If, amongst the collection, there is a 'square' biscuit tin this could open up another field of investigation. Most biscuit tin lids are, in fact, rectangles, although they look square. This means that the lids will only fit on in two ways; if they were square they would fit in four ways. This leads to the questions discussed in Section 6 of this chapter:

Will all squares fit in four ways?

Will all rectangles fit in only two ways?

This gives rise to a discussion of rotational symmetry and one can look at other regular and irregular shapes to see what sort of rotational symmetry (if any) they have. If one moves away from lids with edges to cut-out plane rectangles and squares, then these can be turned over, thus doubling the number of possible symmetries.

Stage IV – The beginning of formalisation

When all the possibilities of the various situations have been explored, there comes a stage at which the children may wish to collect together and formalise what they have learnt. It must be emphasized that this should not come too soon, and for most children this will not be until the fourth year in the primary school or beyond. If, on the other hand, children wish to explore a formal system of classification before this, then they should be encouraged to do so.

4 Classification

When children are investigating the properties of shapes for themselves, definitions tend to evolve rather than suddenly arise in a finished form. This is precisely what has happened in the history of mathematics, where definitions or formulae are continuously being 'improved' as knowledge grows. As an illustration one could again take the case of the square. As has already been pointed out, children know what a square is before they are able to describe it. When asked what makes a figure a square, they might well say, "It has all its sides the same". Until they have seen by moving the jointed strips that it is possible to have a four-sided figure with all its sides equal that is not a square, 'a figure with all its sides equal' can be accepted as a satisfactory definition of a square for the time being. It soon becomes obvious that it has to be modified to exclude those figures that are not squares.

The next step might be 'a figure with all its sides equal and all its angles equal', which in its turn will have to be modified to 'a figure with all its sides equal and all its angles right angles'. One could ask here if these definitions apply to the same figures, or whether they define different figures.

From a purely mathematical point of view, this definition is still not 'perfect' because it now contains too much information. It can be shown that a four-sided figure with all its angles equal has each equal to a right angle, therefore it is sufficient to define a square as a 'four-sided figure with all its sides equal and one angle a right angle'. The logical refinement of seeing that the definition does not carry more information than absolutely necessary is not one that appeals to young children and can be left to a later stage.

The definitions found in many texts are not consistent and it may be helpful for the teacher to be able to see the overall pattern of the classification. The following table should help with this, although it is *not* recommended that it should be given to children in this form. This table is attributed to Poseithorius, an early Greek mathematician, and illustrates the principle of 'classification by dichotomy'. At each fork a decision is made; if a shape possesses the stated property it goes on the left, if not on the right.

Beginning with quadrilaterals, one has

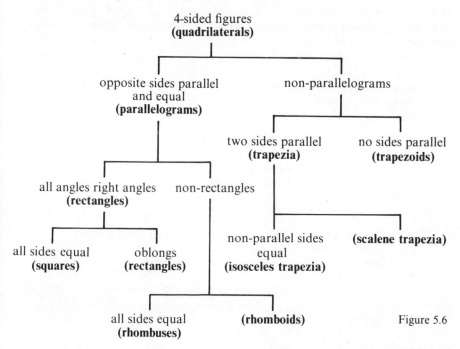

Figure 5.6

In going through this table, it can be seen that the figures have all the properties of whatever has gone before, so that a square has all sides equal, all angles right angles, opposite sides parallel, four sides. A rhomboid does not have all its sides equal, does not have all its angles right angles, but does have opposite sides equal and parallel. One can see, therefore, that rhomboids are all those parallelograms that are not rhombuses, rectangles or squares.

The other most common figure is the 3-sided figure or triangle, and its table goes as follows.

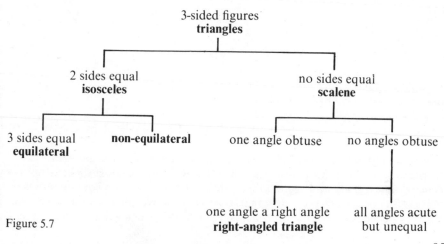

Figure 5.7

95

These classifications depend upon the properties of sides and angles, but there is another very interesting means of classification for quadrilaterals which depends on the properties of the diagonals, providing the figures are convex, i.e. without re-entrant angles.

Diagonals can have any of the following properties:

1 Equal, or unequal
2 Bisect one another; or not bisect
3 Meet at right angles; or not meet at right angles
4 Only one bisected; the other not.

Using these properties, the classification runs as follows

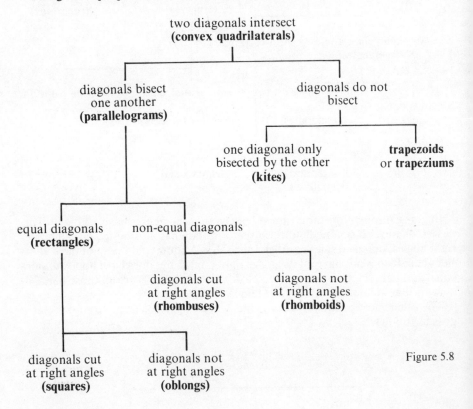

Figure 5.8

(*N.B.* Using the diagonals for classification does not enable us to distinguish the trapezium from the trapezoid.)

When children make up figures with bands on a geo-board, or with jointed strips, they by no means restrict their investigations to the convex figures, and it is important to look and see whether concave figures have similar properties to the convex ones. How many diagonals does the concave quadrilateral have? The answer depends on how the diagonal is defined. If it is defined as a line segment joining two non-adjacent vertices, then the quadrilateral has two non-intersecting diagonals.

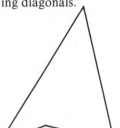 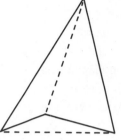

Figure 5.9

This comes as a surprise to many people whose school geometry was confined to convex figures and who, as a result, have assumed that a diagonal must always be inside the figure.

5 Three-dimensional shapes

Only investigations using plane or two-dimensional figures have been discussed so far, although work in three dimensions can be taking place alongside the two-dimensional work all the time. Children from a quite young age live in a world largely filled with three-dimensional objects and good use can be made of this in developing work on shapes.

When studying a particular shape, say a rectangle, a collection can be made of packets and boxes that have rectangular faces. The same can be done with squares and triangles and other shapes. When a collection has been made of these packets and boxes, other ideas connected with them can be investigated. Questions that can be asked include:

How many faces, edges, corners does each have?
Are all the faces the same shape?
What does a cardboard packet look like if it is unfolded and laid out flat?

Besides examining common three-dimensional shapes in order to investigate their properties, they can be fitted together to make further shapes. For instance, those that can be made by fitting together cubes, or cornflake packets of a similar shape and size, can be investigated. For example

How many cubes are needed to make a larger cube?
Can you make a rectangular box shape from 17 cubes?
How many different blocks can be made from 24 cubes?

Three-dimensional shapes can be made by joining together card or plastic plane polygons along their edges with sellotape. This activity again leads to investigation of the possible shapes that can be made. For example

How many squares are needed to make a cube?
Can you make a closed shape with four equilateral triangles?
Can you make a closed shape with four scalene triangles (all the same)?
Can you make a closed shape with more than four equilateral triangles?

The regular solids are made with all the faces the same shape and size. Here are details of a few regular solids for reference.

Name	Faces	Edges	Vertices
Cube	6 squares	12	8
Tetrahedron	4 equilateral triangles	6	4
Octahedron	8 equilateral triangles	12	6
Dodecahedron	12 pentagons	30	20
Icosahedron	20 equilateral triangles	30	12

Most three-dimensional shapes in daily use are, of course, not regular. Most boxes have 6 rectangular faces, not all congruent; a toothpaste tube box often has 4 congruent rectangular faces and two square faces. It is, therefore, important not to restrict investigations to the regular polyhedra.

It will be seen that there is a relationship between the numbers of faces, edges and vertices given in the above table. In fact, if

F = number of faces
E = number of edges
V = number of vertices

then

$$F + V - E = 2$$

This relationship is usually referred to as Euler's theorem for polyhedra. It holds true for *all* convex polyhedra of whatever shape, and children can check it on their collections of packages and containers.

It is also true for many polyhedra that are not convex, but it ceases to be generally true and it is difficult to treat the exceptions systematically. It is true, for example, for a cube with a square hole between two faces, as in the diagram (counting the inner angles as vertices) but it is not true if the hole does not go right through so that the cube appears as a thick-walled box. One would suggest that primary work should restrict itself to convex shapes.

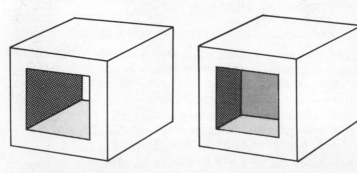

Figure 5.10

Perhaps the commonest container is the cylinder, and this introduces the circular shape, which is itself very common. In any collection of three-dimensional shapes, those with a circular cross-section will appear very frequently and this can lead to investigating the properties of a circle.

One of the problems concerned with work on the circle is that pairs of compasses are by no means easy for young children to use and there is no point at all in investigating a shape which is only approximately a circle. In the lower forms of the Junior School, therefore, it is easier for children to use a tin lid, or other circular object, to draw round when they require a circle. When pairs of compasses are introduced, they can first be used for free pattern making in order to give practice in their use. Patterns of circles, drawn freely and then coloured, can provide a rich experience for children. As with all the other shapes, the concern is not with building up a body of formal knowledge about a circle, but making children aware of the nature of a circle by using it in different ways. The following are some of the intuitive properties of a circle that should emerge.

It is perfectly symmetrical (*any* diagonal is a line of symmetry; any rotation is a symmetry).

There is a fixed point inside it, called the centre, which is equidistant from every point on its perimeter.

All circles are the same shape (but, like squares, can be of different sizes).

6 Symmetry

The ideas of symmetry are very powerful in helping children to classify and analyse shapes. They are essentially intuitive ideas and children recognize symmetry long before they can discuss it. The mathematical meaning of the word is abstracted from the original Greek concept of harmony of proportion, and it is helpful if the teacher is familiar with the different kinds of symmetry.

The simplest and most obvious form of symmetry is symmetry about a line and can be produced by the child using the familiar ink blot pattern.

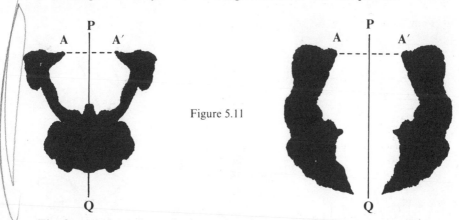

Figure 5.11

The figures show the main features of line symmetry. PQ is the original fold, and the entire figure is symmetrical about this line. Each point A on the left-hand side has a corresponding point or *image point* A' on the other side, and the line joining A and A' is at right angles to, and is bisected by PQ. The left-hand half is the optical image of the right-hand half seen in a mirror held vertically along PQ. If a handbag mirror silvered to the edge is held along this line, the whole shape can still be seen made up of half the shape and its reflection.

99

Familiar shapes may have more than one line of symmetry. Here are some examples.

Lines of Symmetry

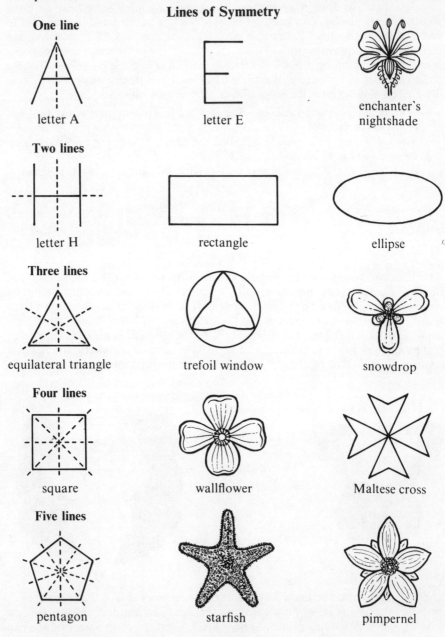

One line		
letter A	letter E	enchanter's nightshade
Two lines		
letter H	rectangle	ellipse
Three lines		
equilateral triangle	trefoil window	snowdrop
Four lines		
square	wallflower	Maltese cross
Five lines		
pentagon	starfish	pimpernel

Figure 5.12

Children can investigate the symmetry of these figures by drawing and folding or by using a mirror.

100

Certain configurations commonly encountered do not possess lines of symmetry. One of these is the letter N. (Many people are not convinced of this until they have actually tried it!) If, however, the N is given a half-turn about the mid-point of the cross line, it fits, and is said to have rotational or cyclic symmetry.

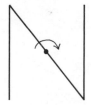

Figure 5.13

The point about which the configuration is rotated is a centre of symmetry.

Here are a few configurations with rotational symmetry. The centres are shown.

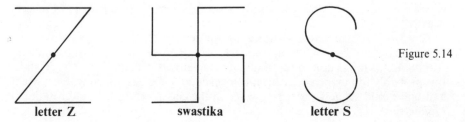

Figure 5.14

letter Z **swastika** **letter S**

Note that the letters S and B as usually printed are not symmetrical at all, since the shape is considered more pleasing if the top half is smaller than the bottom. Some of the previous configurations symmetrical about lines – the square, the rectangle, the ellipse, for example – also possess rotational symmetry.

The number of times that a configuration can be rotated 'to fit on itself' is called the *order* of cyclic symmetry. The letters Z, N and S can each be rotated through half a turn to look identical and have rotational symmetry of order two. The equilateral triangle has three lines of symmetry and exhibits cyclic symmetry of order three. However, the triquetra (more familiar as the three legs in the Manx coat of arms or as a device on Greek shields, where it is called a triskelion) shows cyclic symmetry of order three but has no lines of symmetry.

Figure 5.15

Emblem of Isle of Man

The circle is symmetrical about any diameter and exhibits cyclic symmetry of order infinity.

There is a third kind of symmetry, which is shown by all configurations with an even order of rotational symmetry. This is usually called central symmetry. It can be made clear by the example of a parallelogram.

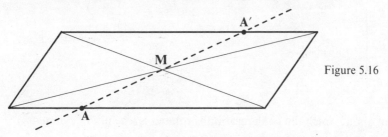

Figure 5.16

This has no line of symmetry, but if *any* line is drawn through the point M where its diagonals intersect, then AM = A′M, where A and A′ are the points where the line (shown dotted) cuts the opposite sides. A tiny mirror at M reflects A as A′.

This kind of symmetry is shown by the letters Z, N, S, the swastika, the hexagon; but not by equilateral triangles, pentagons or the Isle of Man emblem. Although it is important in the study of symmetrical structures such as crystals, it is probably too involved a concept to be suitable for discussion with children, and one would suggest restricting work in the classroom to line and rotational symmetries.

The symmetrical properties of shapes can be investigated by finding the different ways in which they can be fitted into their outlines drawn on paper. If the outline of a cut-out square is drawn on the paper, it can be rotated through a greater turn successively to fit the outline four times.

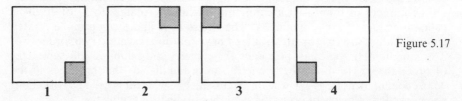

Figure 5.17

The square can also be turned over top to bottom and side to side showing the lines of symmetry that join the mid-points of opposite sides. It will also fit into its outline if turned about both diagonals corner to corner.

A rectangle can only be rotated through half a turn to fit into its outline, giving two positions.

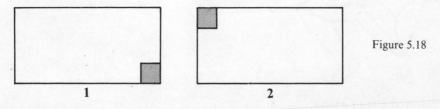

Figure 5.18

The rectangle can also be turned side to side and top to bottom, but if turned over about a diagonal, it does not fit into its outline,

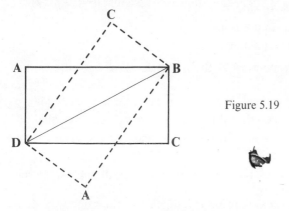

Figure 5.19

so that a diagonal of a rectangle is not a line of symmetry. This fact may be confirmed by folding a rectangle along a diagonal to show that the two halves do not coincide.

The following table collects the symmetries of some common shapes.

Shape or Configuration	Lines of Symmetry	Order of Rotational Symmetry	Central Symmetry
Butterfly	1	1	No
Square	4	4	Yes
Rectangle	2	2	Yes
Triangle (equilateral)	3	3	No
Pentagon	5	5	No
Starfish	5	5	No
Swastika	0	4	Yes
Triquetra	0	3	No
Circle	inf.	inf.	Yes
The letter Z	0	2	Yes

The properties of shapes using their symmetries

By putting together the ideas of symmetry and the movements made with cut-out shapes when they are being tessellated, it is possible to investigate their properties.

If one draws round the outside of a cut-out rectangle:

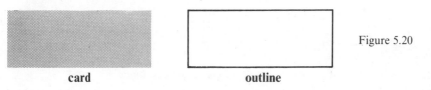

Figure 5.20

card   **outline**

then the rectangle can be fitted into the outline in four ways. In doing this one can use a number of operations.

1 Turn the rectangle side to side.

2 Turn the rectangle top to bottom.

3 Turn the rectangle through half a turn.

As well as showing the symmetries of the rectangle, these movements show various properties.

1 The two short sides are equal, and the corners on the sides are equal.

2 The two long sides are equal, and the corners on the sides are equal.

3 Both pairs of opposite sides are equal and all the angles are equal to one another.

Similarly, with all other shapes, the movement of one side or angle to coincide with another shows their equality.

The properties of the diagonals can be investigated in the same way. If the rectangle is rotated through half a turn, the diagonals are interchanged and therefore are shown to be equal in length.

7 Paper folding

An activity that leads to some interesting investigations of shape is that of paper folding. Books on origami, although they make little reference to the mathematical aspects of the activity, provide a wealth of activities that enlarge the child's experience of shape, and for this reason can be recommended.

There are, however, more specifically mathematical activities associated with the idea of paper folding. The simplest of all is the folded right angle. Take any scrap of paper and make a single fold in it.

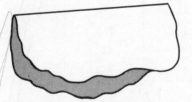

Figure 5.21

Then fold this fold upon itself anywhere along the length

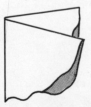

Figure 5.22

and a useful tool for measuring right angles has been made.

It is possible to explore the symmetry of the patterns that arise from different ways of folding by cutting the folded paper into a shape and then opening it out. To predict the pattern that will arise when the paper is unfolded is more difficult than it seems, as the reader can test for himself by trying the following exercise.

Take a rectangular sheet of paper and fold as if folding a right angle.

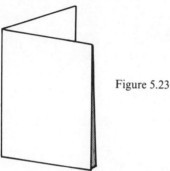

Figure 5.23

Keep the new shape flat and with a pair of scissors cut a pattern out of the face such as

Figure 5.24

Now, *before* opening the paper up, draw what the pattern will look like when the paper is opened. If you are right first time, cut a more complicated pattern and see if you are still successful.

8 Tiling and tessellation

When exploring a shape on a geo-board, the invitation posed by the material is to *change* the shape; to stretch the band to another pin, to add another side, or to make a vertex to another pin. If on the other hand plastic or cardboard geometric shapes are explored, then the invitation is to place them in relation to one another and to explore their properties. The difference makes clear the importance of selecting apparatus for its potential in initiating investigation.

Children will first be concerned with simple pattern-making activities where a number of shapes either congruent or different are fitted together. Once relationships between the shapes have been explored in this way, questions can be asked that will focus attention on certain aspects of the activity.

105

Similar shapes

Given congruent squares and starting with one square one can ask,"How many squares are needed to make the next largest square?"

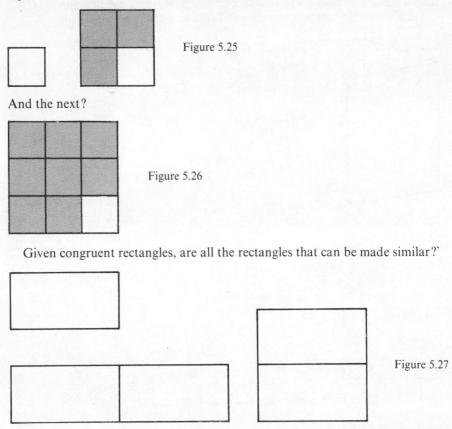

Figure 5.25

And the next?

Figure 5.26

Given congruent rectangles, are all the rectangles that can be made similar?"

Figure 5.27

The two shown are similar neither to one another nor to the original rectangle.

Another question is
"How many equal triangles are needed to make larger triangles similar to themselves?"

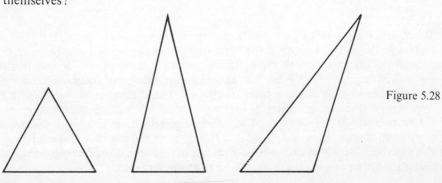

Figure 5.28

Such questions can be asked of any geometrical shape. Sometimes it is not possible to make similar shapes, but when it is possible the square number sequence 1, 4, 9, 16 . . . arises for successive similar figures.

Tessellation

There is a difference between simple pattern-making and tessellation in that a tessellation contains a simple unit which repeats. The units will always fit together without gaps, however many times they are repeated.

A simple pattern like the following

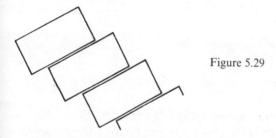

Figure 5.29

will make a tessellation because rows made in this way will fit together.

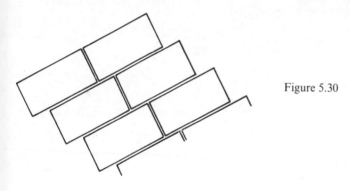

Figure 5.30

A pattern like this, however,

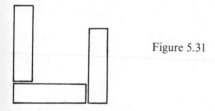

Figure 5.31

will not make a tessellation because the shapes cannot be fitted together to make an all-over pattern.

Some regular shapes such as the pentagon and octagon will not fit together on their own without gaps. The pentagon can be tessellated with the addition of rhombuses and the octagon with the addition of squares.

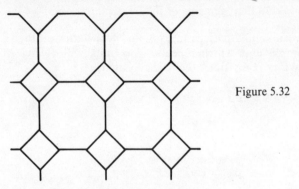

Figure 5.32

Octagons tessellated with squares

It is also interesting to explore the tessellation of irregular shapes. All congruent scalene triangles will tessellate and so will congruent scalene quadrilaterals. The triangles are simple because any two congruent triangles will make a parallelogram

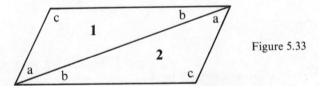

Figure 5.33

but the quadrilaterals are more difficult. If four are fitted together as in the diagram

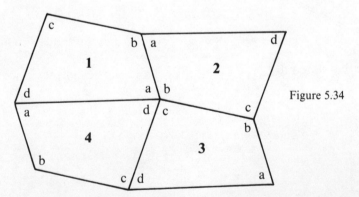

Figure 5.34

it will be found that the blocks of four fit together as a tessellating unit.

The tessellation of irregular shapes is a wide topic that can be narrowed for discussion by considering a limited range. An interesting set of shapes is that of the so-called polyominoes. These are extensions of the familiar domino, which consists of two squares edge to edge. Polyominoes are the general configurations made with 2, 3, 4, 5 . . . squares. The 5-square polyominoes are called pento-minoes. There are twelve possible arrangements of the five squares, all of which tessellate. One is

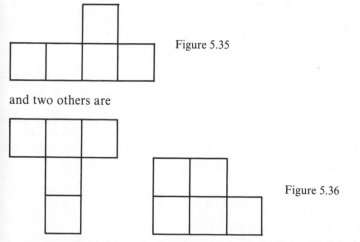

Figure 5.35

and two others are

Figure 5.36

If two of the 'T' shapes are fitted together, then the double shape will tessel-late.

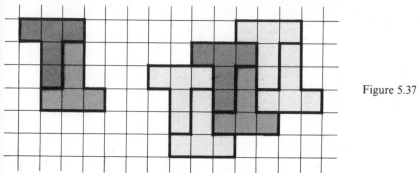

Figure 5.37

If the 'L' shape is placed in rows, then one row can be 'turned upside down' to fit the next.

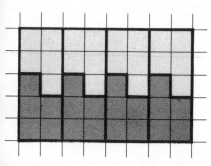

Figure 5.38

One can also explore the possibilities of tessellating with shapes made from a number of equilateral triangles of the same size (called polyiamonds)

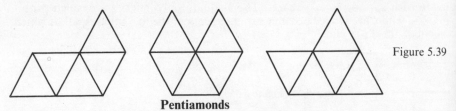

Figure 5.39

Pentiamonds

The advantage of exploring polyominoes and polyiamonds is that they can be made easily from squared or triangle-gridded paper and the results recorded on the paper.

Any grid (or 'lattice') represents a tessellation and the grids can be used for developing further tessellation units. A parallelogram grid can be turned into a different kind of tessellation if each parallelogram is altered in the same way. A parallelogram grid and two examples are shown.

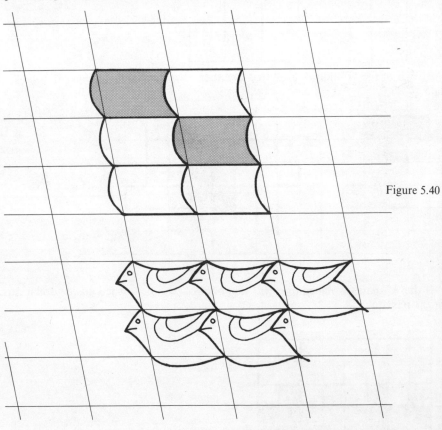

Figure 5.40

Many fascinating tessellation patterns can be developed in this way starting with a triangle, parallelogram or hexagon grid.

9 Points and lines

If a number of lines that cross one another are drawn, they give a configuration made up of the lines themselves together with the crossing points.

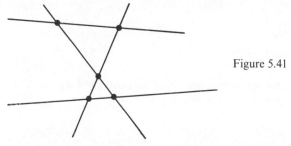

Figure 5.41

Alternatively, a collection of points could be drawn, and then lines drawn through them giving the same configuration. Some configurations of points and lines show the interesting property called *duality*. The dual of a configuration is that obtained by interchanging the words 'point' and 'line' in its description. Thus one has the configuration 'three points on a line'.

Figure 5.42

Its dual is 'three lines on a point'.

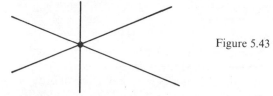

Figure 5.43

This relation is too subtle for discussion with primary pupils.

When the lines have been drawn, they may enclose regions of space and several interesting investigations can be carried out exploring the connection of lines, points and spaces. The configurations so formed are usually referred to as networks.

Most children at some stage come across the 'puzzle' where one is asked to trace a shape without taking the pencil off the paper and without retracing lines.

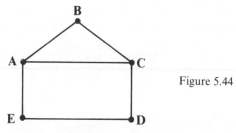

Figure 5.44

Diagrams which it is possible to draw in one continuous line without going over the same line twice are called unicursal. They fall into two separate kinds;

those where the line begins and ends at the same point and those where the line does not come back to the beginning.

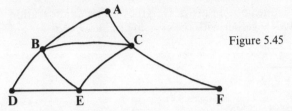

Figure 5.45

The above figure can be drawn starting at any point and will finish at the same point, but the following must start at A and finish at C or vice versa.

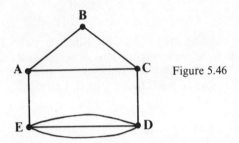

Figure 5.46

It is possible to decide which kind of unicursal diagram it is or if it is in fact impossible to draw in one line by considering the number of paths that run to each point in the diagram.

The points in a network are called *nodes*.

The lines joining them are called *arcs*, and can be drawn straight or curved.

The number of arcs meeting at a node is called the *order of the node*.

In Figure 5.45, nodes A, D, F, are of order 2; nodes B, C, and E are of order 4.

In Figure 5.44, nodes B, E, D are of order 2; nodes A and C are of order 3.

If all the nodes in a network are of even order, then the network can be drawn as one line, starting or finishing at any point, since for each path *into* a node there is a corresponding path *out*. If there is a node of odd order, then eventually one enters the node but cannot proceed. One cannot then complete the diagram *unless the node concerned is a starting or finishing point*. It follows that a configuration with two but not more than two odd nodes is unicursal if, but only if, one starts and finishes at these nodes.

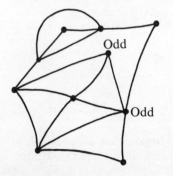

Figure 5.47

The theory of unicursal networks as just explained is not of great importance to children in the primary school, but it is possible for them to investigate these ideas to see what differences they can find in the various networks. One way of doing this is to construct the networks from the constituent parts. Material is available commercially which consists of small plastic rings with projections, the number of projections being the order of the node, and plastic straws with which to join the nodes. Alternatively, different coloured lumps of plasticine can be used for the nodes and joined with plastic drinking straws.

The investigation will be concerned with seeing what kinds of networks it is possible to construct from various collections of nodes. For example,

try to make a network with
  2 nodes of order 2 and 3 nodes of order 4.
Or with
  1 node of order 2, 2 nodes of order 4 and 1 node of order 3
and so on.

When various networks have been explored, it can be seen that networks are only possible with an even number of nodes of odd order, and of these only those with two are unicursal.

10   Regions

When a line is drawn on a plane, it divides it into two regions, as numbered in the diagram.

1

2   Figure 5.48

For a closed network of lines the regions are those formed by the arcs joining the nodes. There will be one region outside the network, while the space inside is divided into smaller regions by the lines.

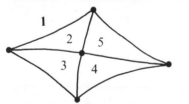

Figure 5.49

If the arcs, nodes and regions in such a network are counted, it will be seen that they have a relation analogous to Euler's theorem discussed earlier on page 98. That is, if

R=number of regions
A=number of arcs
N=number of nodes

then

113

$$R + N - A = 2$$

corresponding exactly to

$$F + V - E = 2$$

As with Euler's polyhedron theorem, there are restrictions. The relation applies to a network which is not closed, but only if no line is of indefinite length. Thus it holds for Figure 5.50

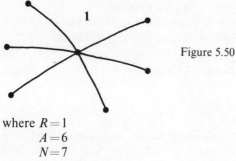

Figure 5.50

where $R = 1$
$A = 6$
$N = 7$

but not for Figure 5.51

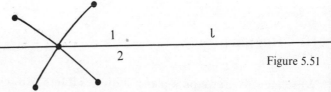

Figure 5.51

where one of the lines divides the plane. In this case

$R = 2$
$A = 6$
$N = 5$

and $R + N - A = 1$

The formula will still hold if we argue that the line l in the diagram is only one arc, but children are likely to remain unconvinced. Another condition is that there must be at least one node. A circle, for the purposes of the formula, must begin and end at a node and not be drawn as a continuous loop.

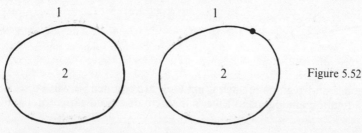

Figure 5.52

For these two figures

$R = 2, A = 1, N = 0$ $R = 2, A = 1, N = 1$

so that the formula only holds for the second.

The configuration must also be entirely connected. The formula holds good for Figure 5.53a but not Figure 5.53b.

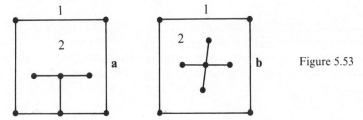

Figure 5.53

The formula will remain true for these exceptions if one counts elements other than regions, arcs and nodes, i.e. if closed circuits without a node are counted as C and unconnected parts of the diagram as U then, for Figure 5.54:

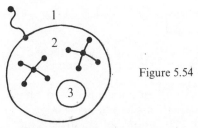

Figure 5.54

$$R=3,\ A=11,\ N=12,\ C=1,\ U=3$$

The formula then becomes

$$R+N+C-A-U=2$$

This will now hold good on *any* diagram drawn with lines which end in the plane. This might be a possible topic for investigation by children with the help of the teacher, but in general, the simpler cases of the connected network with nodes are more suitable for primary work.

A familiar example of a network is an outline map, where the arcs or lines correspond to frontiers or coasts and the nodes to the meeting points of frontiers with coasts or with one another. The regions of a network can be coloured by children in the same way that colour is used on maps, with no two regions in the same colour if they have a common boundary. One can then investigate the minimum number of distinct colours that will serve to colour any map or network. The answer appears to be four. The statement that this is so is the so-called Four Colour Theorem. This is a famous example of an, until recently, unsolved problem in mathematics, but which is still simple enough to be investigated by young children. No one had constructed a map, however improbable in topography, that required more than four distinct colours; but also no one had succeeded in proving that not more than four colours are necessary. It has recently (1976) been proved to be true.

Most maps use more than four colours, of course, to distinguish national or other areas, but four enables one to distinguish frontiers and coasts, including sea and land. Two regions of the same colour can, without confusion, meet at a point.

Children frequently produce what they regard as exceptions, but it is usually fairly easy to see how the fifth colour can be replaced by one already used.

115

11   Angles and bearings

The concept of an angle can present difficulties to young children since it both represents the size of a 'corner' and is a measure of turn.

A useful piece of apparatus for introducing angle to children can be made with two thin card strips, approximately 1 cm × 15 cm, pierced at one end with a paper fastener.

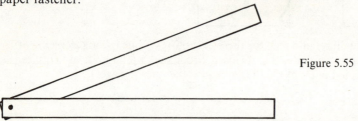

Figure 5.55

If the children hold the strips together and are then asked to open them *at an angle*, they are using the word to fit the correct action, and no more formal definition of angle is necessary.

The strips can then be used to demonstrate 'sharp' or *acute* angles and 'blunt' or *obtuse* angles, with the right angle as the borderline between the two.

It is important that children should realize that the size of an angle is independent of the length of the arms that contain it. In order to demonstrate this, pivoted strips of different lengths can be turned through the same amount and put side by side.

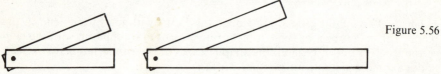

Figure 5.56

For most of the work in the primary school, it is quite sufficient to measure angles in terms of right angles. If a folded right angle is made as described in Section 7, page 104, the paper can be opened flat as in the diagram.

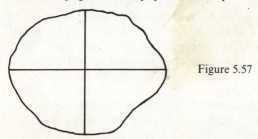

Figure 5.57

Then the folds show four right angles at a point. The paper can then be pinned down by a pin through the point, and rotated. If turning round until the starting point is reached is regarded as a whole turn, then one right angle is a quarter turn and a straight line is a half turn. These measures are quite sufficient for all early work on shape and help children to form the concept of an angle as a measure of the amount of turning.

Should a smaller angle be required, then the folded right angle can be halved giving half a right angle or an eighth of a turn. If the piece of paper that has been folded to make a half right angle is unfolded and placed flat, it will give eight points of the compass.

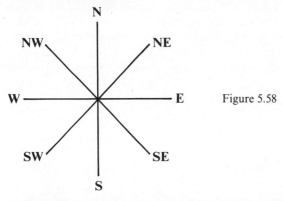

Figure 5.58

The major problems associated with the introduction of the degree as a measure of the angle are the smallness of the unit and the technical difficulty of using a protractor. For these reasons, it is advisable to leave the introduction of the degree till late in the primary school.

The technical problems of using a protractor can be eased by using a transparent circular protractor marked from 0° to 360°, with a centre that can be put accurately over the apex of the angle.

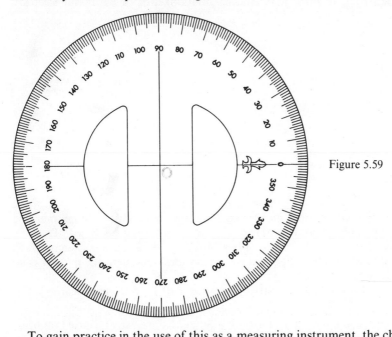

Figure 5.59

To gain practice in the use of this as a measuring instrument, the children can draw angles to a given size and measure angles already drawn.

One application of the use of a protractor that appeals to older primary children is its use to find bearings. All bearings have been standardized internationally to begin at North and to go through 360° back to North. In order to prevent confusion, all bearings are given with three digits starting at 000°.

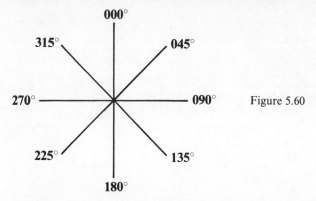

Figure 5.60

A further difficulty is the co-existence of two different accepted conventions for the measurement of angle. Although bearings begin with their zero at North and increase clockwise to 359° before returning to zero, the standard method in mathematics is to take the zero horizontally to the right (i.e. East on a compass) and to measure angles anticlockwise.

Thus the line OA would appear on a bearing 030° in a book on navigation, but at an angle of 60° in most mathematics textbooks, or in books on electrical engineering.

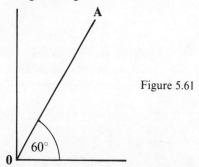

Figure 5.61

In the primary school only the bearing convention need be stressed. For the rest the children are merely measuring the angle between two lines marking directions, and the question of sense of rotation need not be raised. There is, incidentally, a quite obsolete form of bearing angle, the quadrant system, which is still found in older school books at secondary level, but, here again, there is no point in mentioning it in class.

Simple puzzles on finding 'buried treasure' can be set using bearings. For example,

Two trees are 50 m apart on a North–South line and treasure is buried on bearing 047° from the southern tree and 138° from the northern tree. Draw a scale diagram to find where the treasure is buried.

Such an exercise can also be carried out practically in the school grounds.

Some elementary investigation can be made into the properties of the angles of certain figures. If a triangle is cut out and its corners torn off and rearranged, it can be shown that the angles of a triangle together make a half turn.

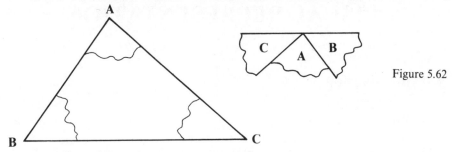

Figure 5.62

It is unlikely, however, that young children would measure the angles of a triangle with a protractor accurately enough to make the total 180°, and the practical demonstration is more convincing.

Similarly, if the corners of any four-sided shape are torn off and arranged together, they will give a whole turn or four right angles. Note that these are empirical demonstrations and are not intended to correspond to the 'Euclidean proofs' of the more traditional secondary school courses.

12 A note on scale drawing

Formal exercises in scale drawing will not play a large part in the work of the primary school. The children cannot achieve the accuracy that the task really calls for, and are not at home with instruments such as dividers and set squares. Informal plans, say of a room in the child's home, are, of course, a different matter. If they have measured a room as, say 5 m by 4 m, they can draw a rectangle to a 2 cm scale and make reasonable approximations to such things as alcoves or chimney breasts. If the plan is drawn on 2 cm squared paper, this will make the actual drawing of the plan much easier.

A more valuable exercise than scale drawing at primary level is the *interpretation* of scale drawings or models. Such questions as the size of a house in a builder's plan, or the actual size of a scale model locomotive or aircraft, or the distance along the High Street from the church to the Town Hall, as shown in the local street map, come much nearer to the use we all make in real life of this important concept.

Chapter 6

VISUAL REPRESENTATION

1 Introduction

One of the commonest numerical activities of young children is collecting data in answer to the 'how many?' question, such as

How many pets have you got?
How many children in the class have dogs?
How many children stay in to dinner?

Often a question will arise which involves comparison –

Do the children in this class have more cats or more dogs?

In order to answer such questions, it is necessary to record the information. This can be done as a table (which will certainly have to include all the pets in the class!)

Number of children with dogs   6
Number of children with cats   8
and so on.

It can also be recorded by means of a picture. This may be one of the various types of graph discussed later, on an arrow diagram, or any kind of diagram that gives a clear picture of the situation recorded.

An important point is that this kind of pictorial representation gives no more information than the original table of data and is merely an alternative way of presenting it which makes the message easier to understand. For this reason, the representation is only useful because it underlines the message. It does not justify collecting data specially for making a graph. It is much better to introduce techniques when the need arises, as it will do from data that the children have collected for their own intrinsic interest.

The following are two examples of the kind of activity that gives rise to pictorial representation. They are put here before a detailed discussion.

1 A group of third year children collecting information about India (which they associated with drought and dryness) came across the statement that a certain village had "one of the largest rainfalls in the world". The rainfall as it was given did not mean very much to them until they had cut strips of paper marked at intervals representing the rainfall in the Indian village and the rainfall for their own and other towns. This led to a great many strips each for a different place. Placed together these strips gave a block graph.

2 A class of first year children were discussing one day how many of the children were brought to school in cars and how many walked. They decided

to record this by making pictures on gummed paper, one for each child who came by car and a different one for each child who walked. These were then stuck together to make a picture of what happened.

Figure 6.1

Someone soon spotted that, although the line with the cars in it was longer there were fewer cars than walkers.

2 Pictograms and symbols

If a school sells milk to the children, the collection of bottle tops forms a convenient tally of the number of bottles consumed in a week, and this could be displayed in a form leading naturally to the graph proper. The wrappers of sweets eaten during break can also be collected, and forms an interesting comment on the eating habits of children.

Figure 6.2

Here the actual tops or wrappers were stuck each day to a large sheet of paper in lines, and one could begin to discuss ways of improving the display. First, one notes that the apparently greater consumption on Monday compared with Thursday is misleading, as a count will show. But one can arrange things so that a glance at the row is sufficient, rather than the laborious task of counting each top. The tops could be fixed in squares previously marked, so that they space evenly and a direct visual comparison is possible.

121

Milk drunk by our group

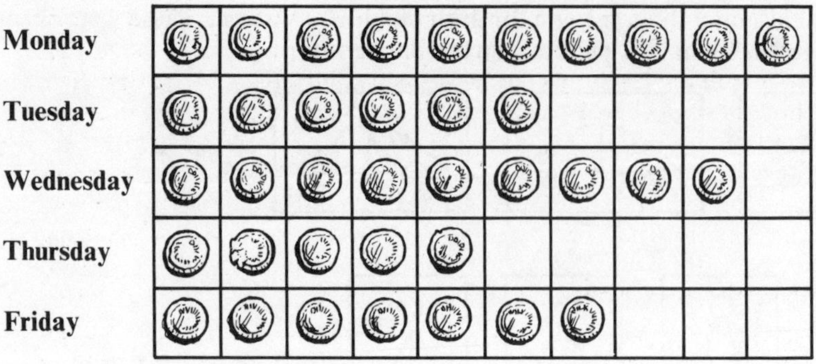

Monday										
Tuesday										
Wednesday										
Thursday										
Friday										

Figure 6.3

It is important that the graph should also be accompanied by a double entry table, listing the days and the bottles consumed; the display and this table are to be considered as parallel records.

Milk drunk by our group	
Day	**Bottles**
Monday	10
Tuesday	6
Wednesday	9
Thursday	5
Friday	7

This process is in effect the collection of trophies – rather like the scalp hunters who thus displayed the numbers of their conquered enemies. It leads to the graph proper by substituting some sort of symbol for the 'trophies'.

To record pets kept by the children, each child who keeps one can draw on a square or disc of gummed paper a cat, dog, goldfish or whatever, and these can be stuck, evenly spaced, after the entries in the column of animals.

Our pets

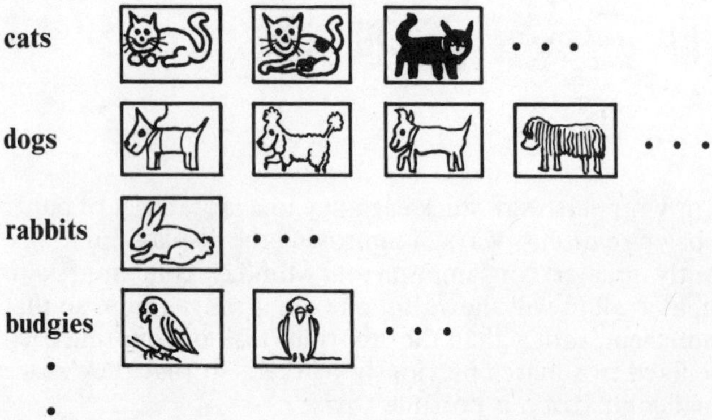

Figure 6.4

122

The symbols here are the child's direct attempt at representational art, however conventionalized they become in the drawing. In a similar way, drawings of cars or buses, or of children walking, illustrate the information on page 121. Another activity involving a whole class is to record birthdays by getting each child to draw himself on a slip of paper, say 5 cm × 8 cm, sticking this in a row next to the correct month.

At the next stage, that of the pictogram, the true representational graph begins to emerge. A pictogram is a conventional pictorial symbol, whose use in conveying statistical information has been made familiar by the 'isotype' diagram. Instead of the individual drawing, a standard and usually highly conventionalized symbol is used. In classroom practice, a stamp can be made as a lino or potato cut. An easy example would be a graph of eye colour. The pictograph stamp would give the outline, and the children could colour in the eye pupils.

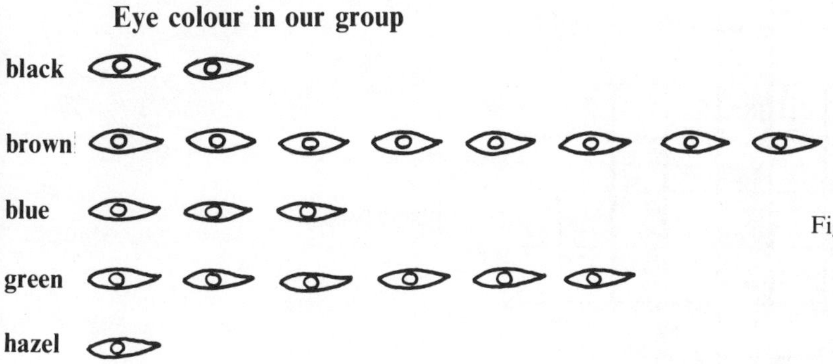

Eye colour in our group

Figure 6.5

If pictograms are of the same size and evenly spaced, the graph allows direct visual comparison. The point is important because children may tend at first to make this comparison, judging the longer line of drawn dogs against the shorter line of budgerigars without noticing which is more numerous. Discussion can ensure that in the end the children space the symbols evenly, probably by using squared paper; otherwise the graph loses much of its value.

As devised by Otto Neurath, the 'isotype' did more than the pictogram since each symbol also carried a numerical value. The extension can be made later, but until the graph is quite familiar to the child, it is easier to use one symbol for each count of one.

3 Block graphs

The information that was contained in the eye chart can also be represented by filling in a square on 1 cm squared paper to correspond to an eye of the colour listed at the bottom of the column. The tabulated information could be

Eye colour of class	
Colour	Number
Black	2
Brown	8
Blue	3
Green	6
Hazel	1

The block graph corresponding to this is

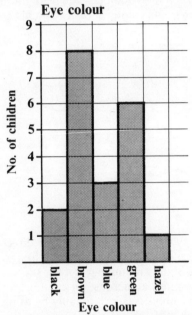

Figure 6.6

What follows is an account of an investigation suitable for third and fourth year children showing how the various kinds of representation can be used.

A 4 cm square hole is cut in a piece of thin card and used to mark a small section of newspaper or a page in a book. The vowels that occur in the passage are counted and recorded.

The initial tabulation can also be done using the orthodox 'five stroke' as a means of counting. The children can be helped to arrive at this scheme by discussing the problem of recording in a neat and unambiguous way.

Vowel count

A ⊞⊞ ⊞⊞ ||| 13

E ⊞⊞ ⊞⊞ ⊞⊞ ⊞⊞ | 21   Figure 6.7

I ⊞⊞ ⊞⊞ || 12

O ⊞⊞ ⊞⊞   10

U ⊞⊞ ⊞⊞ ⊞⊞ | 16

The graph can then be built up on squared paper to give a pattern which a child can compare visually with that obtained by his classmates. It will be found that, using newspaper or magazine articles or pages of ordinary descriptive or narrative prose, the results show a fairly consistent pattern.

The block graph can now be used here instead of drawings or specific symbols. A square is filled in to correspond to each vowel found, and the graph built up, either step by step as the passage is examined, or better, as an illustration of the table of results already recorded.

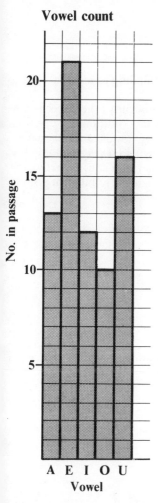

Figure 6.8

So far there has been no mention of scales or axes. This vowel graph now forms a useful lead in to the concept of scale. If a number of groups have each produced a table, the tables can be combined and totalled.

Group	A	E	I	O	U
I	31	38	25	17	11
II	25	46	38	22	12
III	31	38	25	19	11
IV	9	24	9	22	9
V	26	16	9	7	5
VI	25	32	18	13	3
VII	20	20	22	16	6
Totals	167	214	146	116	57

The manipulation of the data in tabulating and totalling is a valuable and practical exercise in addition.

The requirements of the graph at once produce a difficulty; the paper is not big enough to hold the squares. Discussion then leads to a solution, the decision to allow one square to stand for a convenient number of vowels rather than one.

It then becomes worthwhile to adopt a device which saves counting the squares and multiplying, each time the graph is consulted. That is, a reference axis is set up along the columns of squares, from which the number of vowels can be read off directly. This axis now gives the *frequency scale*.

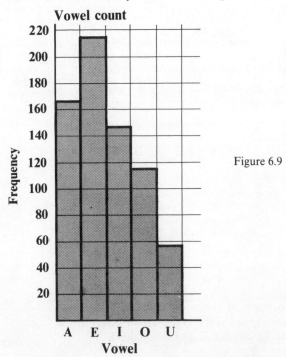

Figure 6.9

The whole exercise has now become difficult and quite sophisticated; it is a genuine investigation with the graph acting as a quick visual reference. The

126

emphasis, however, should be placed on the investigation, not the graph. The graph is only a supplementary tool.

It is interesting to compare English with specimens of French, Italian or other languages, and if as a by-product the children learn to distinguish these from one another, or even to recognize a few words in them, their interest in languages may be aroused. Mathematics taught with constant reference to the real world produces many fringe benefits.

In considering the block graph, there is only one true variable. If attendance is plotted against the five days of the week, then only the attendance can change. Graphs with two variables will be discussed later. The teacher will note that a block or pictogram graph gives a clear visual explanation of the word *average*. If the heights of the columns are evened out by filling in the shorter with squares taken from the longer – this can easily be done if one is using counters or coloured squares – the value corresponding to an even straight line is the *average* or arithmetic mean. There may, of course, be some units left over which cannot be evenly distributed, hence the average often needs to be returned as a fraction. The fraction disappears when the average is multiplied up again to give the total.

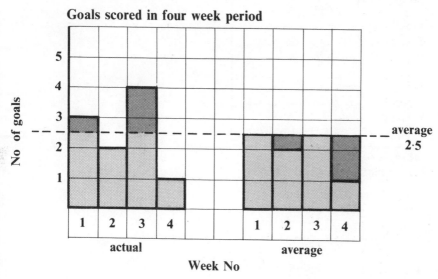

Figure 6.10

4   Frequency distribution graphs

If the heights of a group of children are measured very accurately, they will probably all be different. The data can then only yield useful information if grouped. If the measures are taken to the nearest centimetre, the children will fall into smaller groups differing a centimetre at a time.

In practice one might actually measure to the nearest centimetre, but record the heights as grouped data for illustrating as a block graph, using groups differing by 5 cm or even by 10 cm.

Height (in centimetres)	Number of children
Below 109	3
110–119	12
120–129	11
130–139	4
140 and above	0

If children are asked to record how many children there are in their families, the results can be tabulated as before:

Name	Children in family
Ann	3
Bill	1
Cecil	2
Doreen	4
Edward	1
Francis	2
George	2
Hilary	1

There is the simple block graph.

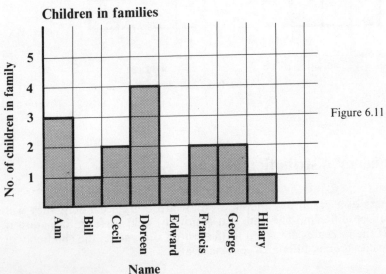

Figure 6.11

128

But one could ask instead how many families there were with 1 child, 2 children, 3 children and so on. The table would then look like this

Number of Children	Number of Families
1	3
2	3
3	1
4	1

The graph would become

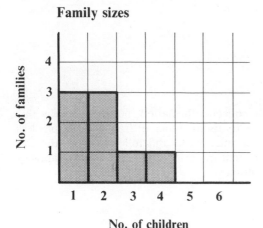

Family sizes

Figure 6.12

No. of families

No. of children

This is called a frequency distribution graph because the original table records the frequency with which 1 appears, 2 appears and so on.

This type of graph is very common in newspapers, advertisements, etc. Children are sometimes worried by it because

1 it does not represent the original data, but data derived from that originally collected, and

2 there is a loss of identity.

It is impossible from the second graph to say how many children there are in Ann's family, but she has a column to herself in the first.

There is a convention which applies to all the later work in this section. If one decides to record traffic passing a given point during a given interval, one can choose the interval but not the flow of traffic. The flow will depend on the time, but the time does not depend on the flow.

Both time and flow change, and are thus called *variables*, but the time is an *independent* and the traffic flow a *dependent* variable. Where this holds good, the established convention is that the independent quantity is laid out along the horizontal axis, the dependent along the vertical. Thus, for a block graph of traffic flow, one would have

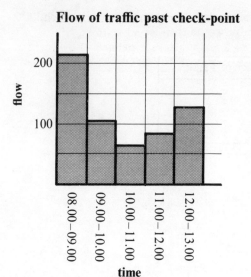

Flow of traffic past check-point

Figure 6.13

Very early graphs, which merely collect information, need not follow this convention, but once the pupil begins to discuss block or frequency graphs less informally, the convention should be introduced and followed. For any frequency graph, the count is the dependent quantity, and hence block graphs of frequency are drawn with vertical columns.

5 Graphs of relationships

The block and frequency graphs have long been familiar in classrooms. There are, however, more general diagrams also regarded as graphs. Children may record relationships by joining (using arrows) entries on two lists which enumerate two sets. In class, one of these would usually be a list of names. Here, for example, a set of five children are linked to the set of days in the week by arrows which read 'was born on'.

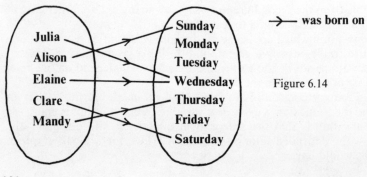

→— was born on

Figure 6.14

Such representations are now common among young children from the time they can read the entries on the lists.

The use of the arrow leads at once to a more abstract picture of a binary relation, which makes clear its equivalence to a verbal statement in the form 'subject – verbal phrase – object'. Consider the statement:

Rosamund is the sister of Stephen.

This can be shown diagrammatically as

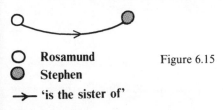

○ **Rosamund**   Figure 6.15
◉ **Stephen**
→ **'is the sister of'**

This representation will be called an 'arrow diagram' although in a full mathematical treatment it is called graphs. A graph is not necessarily a plot of points on squared paper.

If a set of dots represents a set of children, and arrows, coloured or dotted if necessary to distinguish them, represent a set of possible relationships, more complicated arrow diagrams arise.

Thus, if the arrow reads 'is the brother of', one could have

Figure 6.16

From this diagram it can be seen that there are at least two boys (the dots from which the arrows leave). The other members of the set could be boys or girls.

Now take the same diagram but this time suppose that the set is a set of boys.

Figure 6.17

This diagram is now incomplete; we know that brotherhood is a two-way relationship and so the diagram should be

Figure 6.18

131

The diagrams can provide interesting material for class discussion, since they suggest questions that can be followed up. For example, given that the set of dots below represents either boys or girls, and that the arrow reads as before,

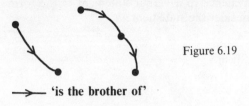

Figure 6.19

—→— 'is the brother of'

1 Which dots **must** represent boys?

2 What arrows **must** be added for completion?

3 If two of the dots represent girls, identify them and complete the diagram.

If one takes a relation such as 'is the son of' then this will lead to other relations as below, using coloured arrows or dotted lines.

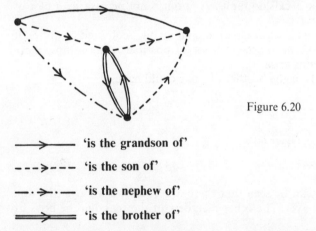

Figure 6.20

——————→—————— 'is the grandson of'

- - -→- - - 'is the son of'

—·—→·— 'is the nephew of'

===⇒=== 'is the brother of'

The only arrow going both ways is 'is the brother of' because this is the only 'reversible' relation. 'Is the son of' reverses into 'is the father of' which is a different relation. It is usually called the 'inverse relation'.

When an arrow is used on a set in this way, it is very important that the relation for which the arrow stands should be clearly understood, and preferably recorded in a legend.

As the idea of arrow diagrams becomes familiar through using them to link up the members of sets, it can be extended to show relationships between numbers. In this case the relation can often be written above the arrow, although some teachers may still prefer a separate legend. For example

Figure 6.21

The statement now reads 'three add four makes seven'.

Given any set of numbers and any two members of it, there is usually more than one possible relation between them. Consider the following:

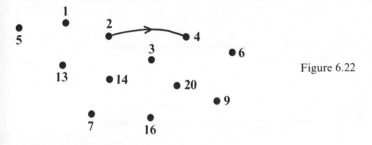

Figure 6.22

Here some possible readings of the arrow are

'add two is'
'doubled is'
'squared is'.

If further arrows are added the reading begins to lose its ambiguity.

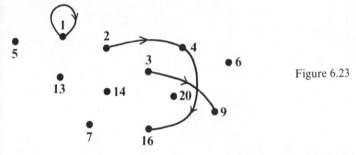

Figure 6.23

It is now clear that the arrow reads 'squared is'. Note that this graph joins 1 to itself by a loop, since 1 squared is 1. Such a relationship, which is like that of the reflexive verb in English (compare 'I wash the dishes' with 'I wash myself') is called *reflexive* and is characterized by the looped arrow. By using arrows of different colours for the other possible relations more complicated diagrams are generated, but since these are easier to draw than to interpret, children usually enjoy making them. If the several relationships are to be discussed further it is better to plot them on separate diagrams. Note that in general the *direction* of the arrow is important. If →— reads 'doubled is' then —← must read 'halved is'.

In the diagrams given, the numbers have been represented by randomly placed dots. The arrow diagrams can still be drawn if the numbers are arranged on a line or in arrays as on a 100 board. When this is done, since the numbers themselves form a pattern, the arrows develop other patterns which can lead to interesting investigations. Consider the arrow 'doubled is' applied to the number line.

Figure 6.24

133

This at once raises the question of why there are no arrows arriving at 3 and 5, and shows how the steps lengthen as one goes along the line.

Another representation uses two number lines instead of one, giving a different pattern which has the same abstract structure linking the same numbers.

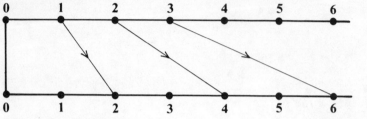

Figure 6.25

The relation 'doubled is'

If one of the two lines is turned so that it is at right angles to the other, intersecting it at the point labelled zero, one gets a representation which is much more like what is usually taken to be a 'graph'. One new feature is seen in that the arrows are now parallel.

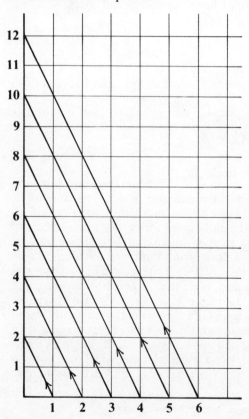

Figure 6.26

The relation 'doubled is'

134

Note that in Figure 6.24 the relation is given as between the members of a set; in the other figures it is seen as one between pairs of numbers, one from each of two sets.

It is now possible to see that the arrow diagram graphs for pairs of numbers correspond exactly to statements involving two place-holders, as introduced in the form

$$\square + \triangle = 6$$

given at the end of Chapter 2. The statement

$$2 + \square = \triangle$$

sets up a relation between the pairs of numbers that fill the place-holders. Thus the pairs

(3, 5), (4, 6), (5, 7) . . .

all fit this statement and correspond to

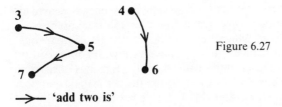

Figure 6.27

⟶ 'add two is'

It follows that the arrow graph is also equivalent to a tabulated set of values. Note that the arrow, by showing a direction, puts the two numbers in order within the pair. It is always taken that the number written first is read first, so that (3, 5) is not the same as (5, 3). Such a pair of numbers enclosed in brackets is usually called an 'ordered pair'.

6   Co-ordinate systems

The idea of a co-ordinate system is an essential concept in the development of other kinds of graphs.

To fix a point on a surface two measures are needed. These can be latitude and longitude, as on the earth's surface, easting and northing as on an ordnance map, bearing and distance off as in navigation, row and seat number as on the seating plan of a theatre.

A convenient practical approach is given by a theatre plan, which can easily be adapted to the layout of desks or chairs in a classroom. Here the rows are lettered and the seats in each row are numbered. It is easy for children to make a seating plan of their classroom on this basis, and to give each child his reference letter and number. The set of all available pairs form a *co-ordinate system*; it enables each seat to be identified and allocated uniquely.

Another practical way also incorporates an interesting class investigation. An ordinary seed box of soil about 30 cm × 40 cm is divided into squares by threads stretched on panel pins driven into the edge at 3 cm intervals. The dimensions given yield over 100 intersections, but the number should not be less than 100. The divisions should be marked as in the diagram.

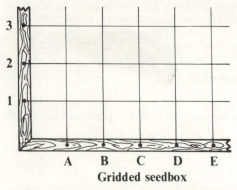

Figure 6.28

Gridded seedbox

Each child then takes 2 or 3 turnip or radish seeds from a packet provided, and with a matchstick pushes each one just below the soil at chosen intersections (one seed per intersection) which he notes down, the letter first, thus: B1, C4, D2. The box is then watered and put in a convenient warm cupboard till the seeds begin to germinate, and each pupil can follow the fortunes of his own seeds. He naturally uses the horizontal axis letter before the vertical axis number (as in the familiar road classification) and this habit serves him in good stead when, later, he uses numbers on the horizontal axis as well. The experiment is described here only to introduce the idea of a co-ordinate system, but clearly, if exactly 100 seeds are planted, the box provides a valuable introduction to percentages and an interesting investigation of the germination characteristics of various seeds.

Another approach is given by a hypothetical city of the future with streets on the New York model, forming a square grid, and such a model can serve as the transition from the letter-number pair to the number pair proper, in which the first co-ordinate is taken to be the direction from west to east (easting).

Street plan (i)

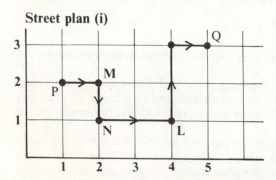

Figure 6.29

In the diagram, a walk beginning at the point (1, 2) finishes at (5, 3), passing through intermediate street corners such as (4, 1). It is interesting to find out what is the shortest possible distance from corner P to corner Q, and whether a finer network of streets between P and Q, as in plan (ii) could alter this shortest distance.

136

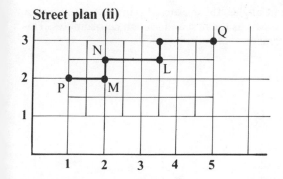

Street plan (ii)

Figure 6.30

The diagram has, however, another use. The corner M is still (2, 2), but what is N? Discussion could produce the suggestion $(2, 2\frac{1}{2})$ and one then readily accepts rational co-ordinates, labelling L for example as $(3\frac{1}{2}, 2\frac{1}{2})$.

It is important at this point to establish the mathematical convention that the horizontal distance is read first, so that (2, 3) means 2 along and 3 up and not the other way. It is perhaps unfortunate that the theatre seat convention is to give the row first. The pupil will, in fact, meet both, but in the context of his work in mathematics, he must learn to stick to one of them. The convention, also used by the National Grid References on Ordnance Survey maps is first reading the distance east, then secondly the distance north. Latitude and longitude, however, go the other way.

Each convention was established as needed and has always worked satisfactorily in context; it is only when one tries to make a generalized abstraction such as that of a co-ordinate system that the clashes appear.

7   Discrete and continuous Cartesian graphs

The two previous sections have shown the representation of a statement involving ordered number pairs and the use of co-ordinates to picture a relationship. The two combine to give the most common form of graphical representation, the Cartesian graph, so called in honour of the seventeenth century mathematician and philosopher, René Descartes. For example, the statement

$$2 \times \square = \triangle$$

gives the table of ordered pairs

$\square$	$\triangle$
1	2
2	4
3	6
4	8

Using two number lines at right angles, these ordered pairs can be shown as points, taking numbers within the pair as the first and second co-ordinates. This gives a representation of the statement

$2 \times \square = \triangle$

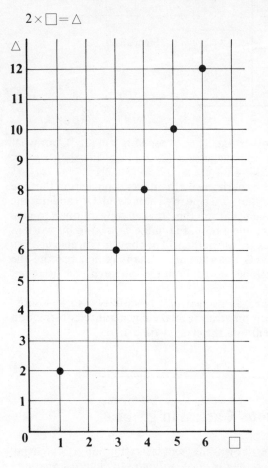

Figure 6.31

The statement itself becomes the title of the graph.

Note particularly that if only whole numbers are being considered, the graph consists of a set of discrete points. A continuous line only occurs if intermediate values are possible. A brief mention of fractional co-ordinates has been made on page 137 but the first graphs drawn by children should be of this discrete form. Drawing a line through the points should be a deliberate decision based on discussion.

If the numbers on the axes represent real objects, the graphs may remain theoretically discrete. Population statistics can only be in integers. Yet it soon becomes clear that, if large numbers are to be represented in the graph, the scale chosen does not allow small or unit increases to be recorded.

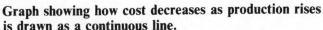

Graph showing how cost decreases as production rises is drawn as a continuous line.

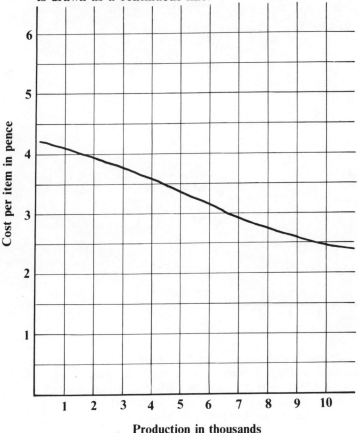

Figure 6.32

Cost per item in pence

Production in thousands

The discrete points then appear to run together as a line, and can be so drawn. Nevertheless, the discrete points that represent, for integers,

$2 \times \square = \triangle$

in Figure 6.31 do lie on a straight line through them even if this line is not drawn in the actual diagram.

In fact, all statements of the form

$n \times \square = \triangle$

where n is *any* number, give points on a straight line, and so do statements like

$\square + n = \triangle$

For this reason, all relationships of the types considered are classed as *linear* relationships.

Yet another linear relationship is

$$\square + \triangle = 6$$

which is represented by the graph shown below.

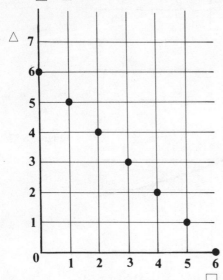

$$\square + \triangle = 6$$

Figure 6.33

Conversely, if one begins with a double entry table of values for $\square$ and $\triangle$, the discovery of a straight line plot allows the conclusion that the relationship is linear. Given the graph, the statement can be written down, although this is a much more difficult exercise than making up a table and plotting when the relationship is known. Here is an example of such a table.

$\square$	$\triangle$
1	0
2	4
3	8
4	12
5	16
6	20

It will be seen that for regular increases in the $\square$ value of the table the $\triangle$ value also increases regularly. This is the number pattern corresponding to a straight line graph or a linear relationship. The actual statement here is

$$(4 \times \square) - 4 = \triangle$$

and this is by no means obvious from inspection of the table. Yet one can at once identify the table as that of a linear relationship, either by drawing the graph or noting the form of the number pattern.

140

Pupils will eventually learn to handle non-linear relationships which, plotted on Cartesian co-ordinates, give points lying on curves. An example of such a relation is

   $\square \times \square = \triangle$

(where, of course, the same number is put in the two box symbols)

   or $144 \div \square = \triangle$

Here 144 is chosen because it has a fairly large set of divisions which do not leave remainders. (See page 142.)

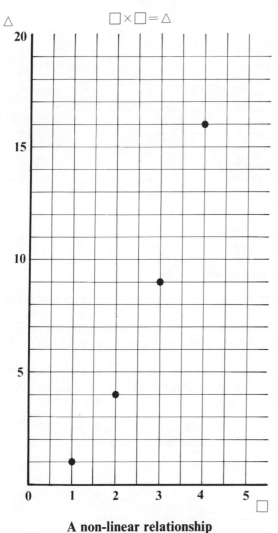

Figure 6.34

A non-linear relationship

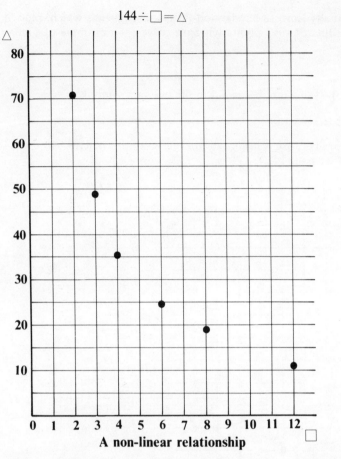

$$144 \div \square = \triangle$$

A non-linear relationship

Figure 6.35

The extension of the graph to record relations between numbers other than whole numbers, so that one has definitely continuous curves or negative co-ordinates, is best done as the extended number systems are studied. The properties of the lines as drawn provide an intuitive parallel with the properties of the numbers.

It is easy to obtain a graph which is not a continuous line. If one plots the postal charges for parcels against their mass, one gets the diagram, derived from the table below taken from Post Office Leaflet PL(B) 3135 of March 1975.

Mass in kg not exceeding	Cost in pence	Mass in kg not exceeding	Cost in pence
1	37	6	82
2	48	7	89
3	57	8	96
4	66	9	103
5	74	10	109

Note the force of the phrase 'not exceeding'.

In mathematics one would use the phrase "less than or equal to" and use the symbol

In the box notation, the first entry in the table could be written

As the mass of the parcel approaches 1 kg, the graph continues as a horizontal line corresponding to the charge 37p, but jumps suddenly to 48p. It is not possible to have a package costing 40p, although the mass itself can vary continuously.

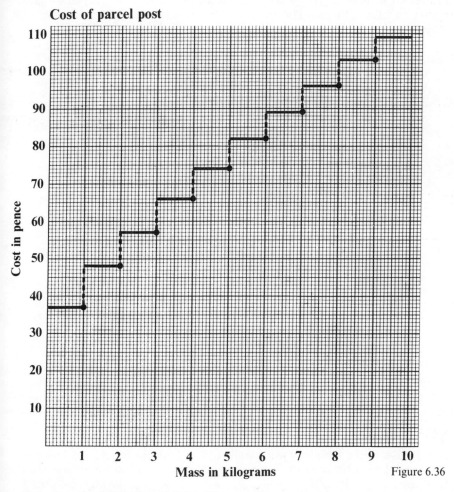

Figure 6.36

Note that the dotted lines in the diagram mean nothing; they merely serve to guide the eye. The heavy dot at one end of each line shows which of the two apparent values has to be chosen; this dot is the visual representation of the symbol in this context.

8 Line graphs from data and experiment

The representation by Cartesian co-ordinates discussed in the previous section is commonly used as a means of recording physical experiments. There is a considerable difficulty in developing this form of representation, and the difficulties of planning the graphs are often paralleled by those of obtaining reliable experiment results. Children are unlikely to gain much from plotting experimental observations before they have had experience both in drawing graphs and in performing the experiments accurately.

The convention that the dependent variable takes the vertical axis is important in this work, since it will be found in all the applications of graphical mathematics in other studies. The following are some of the topics that can be investigated in schools and recorded on graphs.

Situation	Independent variable	Dependent variable
Pendulum	Length of string	Time of 50 swings
	Mass of bob	Time of 50 swings
Spring	Mass suspended	Stretch
Lath clamped at one end	Distance of supported mass from clamp	Vertical deflection of free end
Bouncing ball	Height fallen	Height bounced
Electric train	Setting of controller	Time for one circuit of track
Punctured can	Head of water	Volume of water escaping in 20 seconds

These are sophisticated uses of graphs, and the teacher will need to be aware of the ideas involved if the children are not to draw wrong conclusions from their work.

Where the number relationships and their graphs have been thoroughly understood, children who make sufficient progress in handling these physical experiments will notice that some of the results are similar to the number pair relationships already studied. The graph of the swing of the pendulum, for example, has a similar shape to the graph of the squares relationship. This recognition of the similarity will enable it to be said that for practical purposes, the pendulum behaves in this way. It is important, however, to realize that the mathematical relationship is being used as a 'model' for the physical one. The relationship has not been 'proved' from the practical data.

Children when doing experiments are often inaccurate, and it is obviously a mistake to tell a child that there is a linear relation when the points on the graph are patently nowhere near a straight line. For most springs, elastic bands, etc.

the relationship is only proportional for parts of the stretch and a graph like the one below is common for an elastic band.

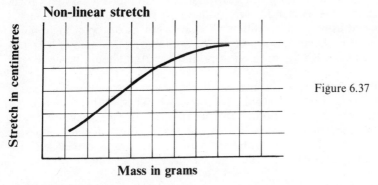

Non-linear stretch

Figure 6.37

The experiment is worth doing because the apparatus is simple and the graph can be used to calibrate the elastic band and use it as a spring balance. But it certainly will not enable the deduction of a general physical law that the extension is proportional to the mass attached.

The important aspect of this work is that children should realize that the picture they get when they draw a graph depends on many things; the accuracy with which they take the readings; the materials used (what the ball that is bounced is made of, or of what wood the lath that is bent); that the experiment itself can introduce variations in readings, e.g. a clockwork train (in the days when children played with them!) ran faster when fully wound than when the spring had almost run down.

In these circumstances, it is important that the graph should be a *true* record of the experiment carried out rather than a forced fit to the known result of a perfect experiment carried out in ideal conditions.

Misunderstanding may follow the use of line graphs in inappropriate situations. A familiar example is the temperature graph.

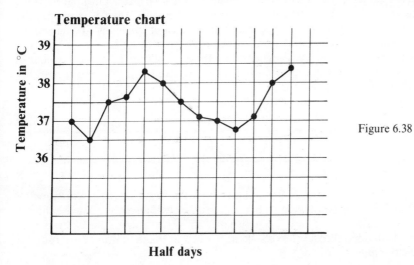

Temperature chart

Figure 6.38

Here the points are discrete and a bar graph would be required in the class-room. All that the lines do is to lead the eye from one point to the next. It is perfectly acceptable in context as in a hospital chart, but for the pupil it carries the suggestion that the temperature varies smoothly from point to point. Such a graph can be confusing to the children who have been used to plotting discrete points. On the other hand, this is accepted as a standard procedure in hospitals and cannot be ignored. If introduced at primary level, it should be done with caution.

Where a line graph is used for interpolation, the assumption is made that the intermediate points, if plotted, would lie on the line. Whether this is true or not depends on the physical situation. It follows that the use of a graph to obtain results not included in the original data, by reading intermediate values, is something that should be done with care. Nonsensical results can arise if it is assumed that all graphs can be treated in this way.

9 A note on the nomogram

The nomogram or alignment chart is familiar in the technical world, but is not often used in schools. It is a form of graph designed for use in reading off results, such as conversions to metric units, in the easiest possible way. In the primary school only very simple examples are investigated, but they are important in that they can replace much of the unsatisfactory work on 'conversion graphs' that is still commonly found.

The line graph plotting miles against kilometres or Fahrenheit degrees against Celsius is a good example of misused graphical methods. To plot one physical quantity against another to see if the results appear to lie on a straight line is a useful process, but to do this when one is merely measuring the same thing in two different units is a waste of time. The graph *must* be a straight line. If, however, the graph is to be used for conversion of the units, then it is inefficient. Interpolation on a graph with the usual axes at right angles is an inaccurate process, requiring vertical and horizontal lines either to be drawn or guessed. The obvious and simple way is suggested by the mile/kilometre stickers available for windscreens from the motoring organizations, and this device of a parallel scale is the simplest nomogram.

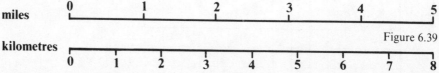

Figure 6.39

Note that drawing the nomogram has required a useful exercise in arithmetic. Given that 5 miles is equivalent to 8 kilometres, how long must a line be so that it can divide easily into 5 and 8 equal parts? In the example, the line is 10 cm long, and is divided into 8 intervals each of 1·25 cm for the kilometres, and 5 of 2 cm for the mile scale.

146

Another form is illustrated in Figure 6.40.

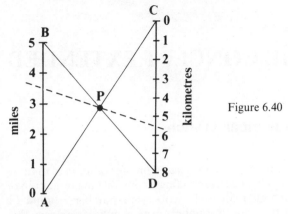

Figure 6.40

Dotted line shows 3½ miles = 5·7 km.

Here two parallel lines AB and CD are drawn. AB is marked in 5 equal units of any convenient length, CD in 8 equal units of any length. The points are numbered 0–5 and 8–0 (in the opposite direction). A point P is marked where the lines joining the two zeros and the end points cross (the lines are shown lightly in the diagram). A transparent ruler put through P and any point on AB or CD gives the corresponding point on CD or AB. The range can be extended by marking 10 and 16 points, or any numbers in the ratio 5:8.

Teachers will see that the nomogram uses the properties of similar triangles. Children are unlikely to follow an explanation but clearly the nomogram is forming a useful bridge between structural pattern and numerical calculation.

An interesting variant of the nomogram can be made from purely numerical relations using parallel scales as before. One could, for example, connect each number in one scale with a given multiple of it on the other. The figure below illustrates the relationship clearly.

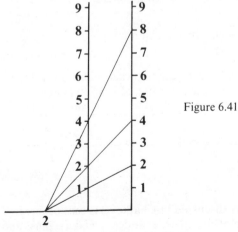

Figure 6.41

Nomogram for multiplication by 2

Chapter 7

NUMBER : THE CONCEPT EXTENDED

1 Extensions to the number system

As discussed in Chapter 2 the number system is based on the counting of discrete objects, the operations with numbers corresponding to possible manipulation of the objects. In recommending that all early work with numbers should be restricted to operations with the natural numbers, one is only keeping mathematics firmly anchored in the objective world.

As mathematics developed, it became necessary to allow the word 'number' to include entities whose properties were not restricted to those associated with discrete objects, and to extend the operations of arithmetic to deal with them. For example, addition visualized as 'counting on' does not apply to fractions. One can demonstrate $3+5=8$ with a few pebbles, but how can one demonstrate $\frac{3}{10}+\frac{1}{6}=\frac{7}{15}$?

In passing from the natural numbers to fractions, there is an increase in abstraction that makes greater demands on the child's understanding. Each extension to the number system is marked by this extension of demand, and restricts the work available to primary schools accordingly. The number systems discussed in this chapter will be those recommended for thorough investigation in class, and not those whose full treatment should await later stages in mathematical education. These recommended numbers and processes, apart from the operations with natural numbers already discussed, are

1 positive and negative signed integers (directed numbers)

2 addition and subtraction of these

3 multiplication of the signed integers by natural numbers

4 positive rationals (fractions).

The modular residue system of numbers for the naturals is also given for its intrinsic interest, and the light it sheds on the recording of time and date.

No other numbers or processes need be introduced into a primary course.

2 Directed numbers

One extension of the natural numbers discussed in Chapter 2 is that of directed numbers, or signed integers. The use of the signs $+$ and $-$ (read as 'plus' and 'minus') as prefixes for numbers has often produced confusion.

148

The modern term 'directed number' is based on a simple representation using number lines or scales and suggests a teaching sequence for introducing them.

1 Note that rulers, thermometers and other scales begin at zero and count units in sequence – that is, the numbers are read in a fixed direction.

2 Ask what would happen if one wanted to read units in the opposite direction, to the left of, or with a thermometer below, the original zero.

3 Agree to a convention that a zero can be anywhere on a line or scale with symbols to distinguish readings left or right of zero.

4 Construct a number line as a scale with a central zero and mark the directed numbers using the agreed symbols for units stepped off to left or to right.

There is a modern convention very suitable for teaching purposes. A forward count of six units is written

$^+6$

and read 'positive 6', a backward count is written

$^-6$

and read 'negative 6'.

This is *not* $+6$ (plus 6) or -6 (minus 6).

The diagram is

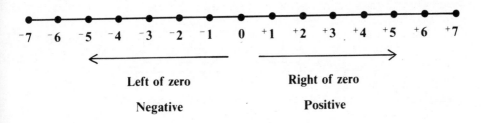

Figure 7.1

Note that the notation given distinguishes clearly between a signed number and the operation of subtraction, and that the brackets used with the standard notation are unnecessary.

Instead of $+3-(-2)$ one has

$^+3-{}^-2$

read as 'positive 3 minus negative 2'. It is suggested that the notation should be used throughout early stages in teaching.

The modified 100 strip can now be used to establish the rules for addition and subtraction.

149

Addition is quite straightforward, since one uses the strips almost as before, but counting on to the right from the zero for a positive addend and to the left for a negative. The figure shows four results.

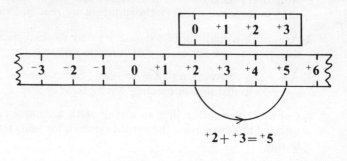

$$^+2 + {}^+3 = {}^+5$$

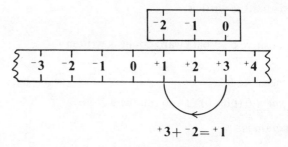

$$^+3 + {}^-2 = {}^+1$$

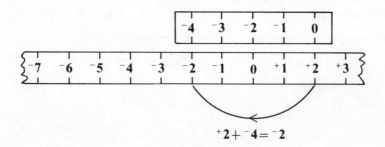

$$^+2 + {}^-4 = {}^-2$$

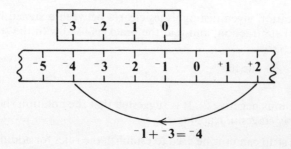

$$^-1 + {}^-3 = {}^-4$$

Figure 7.2

With the strips, subtraction of the negative number intervals is similarly demonstrated. In subtracting natural numbers, one starts to count back on the subtrahend strip *towards* the zero, and this is also done for the positive integers,

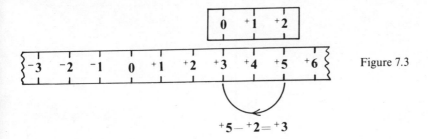

Figure 7.3

exactly as for $5-2=3$.

In demonstrating subtraction of the negative integers, one does the same thing, counting from the last digit again towards the zero. But one is now moving from left to right, so that this is illustrated as

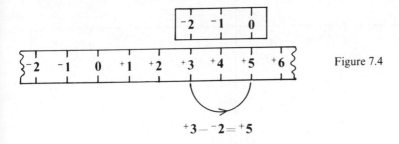

Figure 7.4

The final result is shown in the next figure.

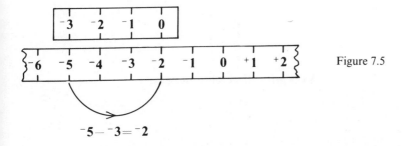

Figure 7.5

It will be seen that the result

$$^+3-{}^-2={}^+5$$

is obtained by reference to the number strip and not by a rule. With practice, children may come to write such results directly.

An early use of directed numbers can be to extend the Cartesian graphs discussed in Chapter 6. Instead of two number lines at right angles beginning at zero, one considers two modified lines as described on page 149 intersecting at zero.

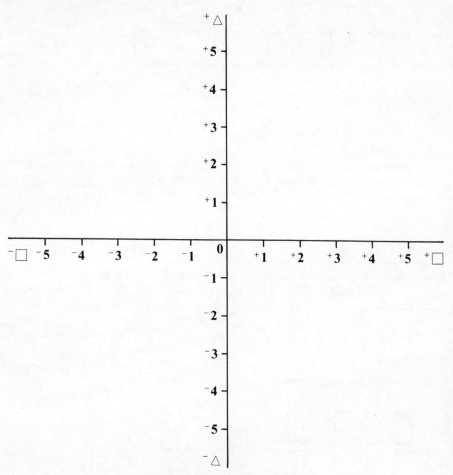

Axes with directed numbers

Figure 7.6

Instead of marking the points 0, 1, 2 . . . they are marked

. . . $^-3$, $^-2$, $^-1$, 0, $^+1$, $^+2$, $^+3$ . . .

and the corresponding ☐ and △ labels are distinguished as

$^+$☐, $^-$☐, $^+$△, $^-$△

as shown in the figure.

The example given in Figure 6.33 can now be extended, as shown

$$\square + \triangle = 6$$

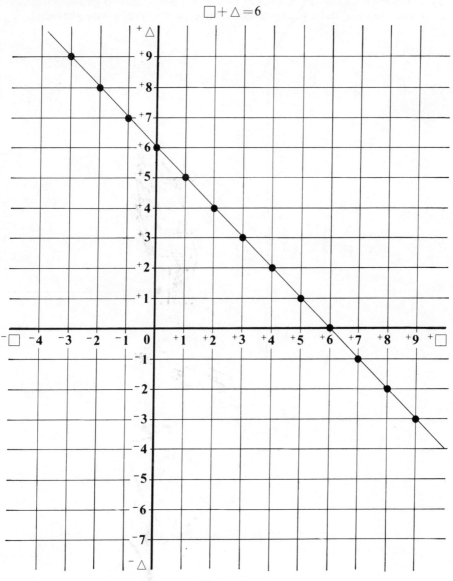

Figure 7.7

Note that including the negative axes extends the straight line, which is no longer confined between its original end points. The use of such an extended graph also makes clear the result of completing statements such as

$$2 \times \square = \triangle$$

with signed numbers.

It is reasonable to take it that 2 lots of ⁻3, since ⁻3 can be represented by 3 steps to the left, is ⁻6. If Figure 6.31 of Chapter 6 is extended in this way, then once more the original line of points extends, but is not otherwise altered.

$2 \times \square = \triangle$

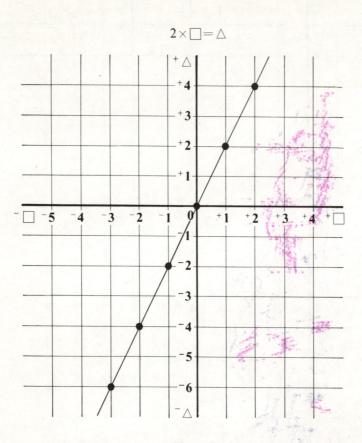

Figure 7.8

Hence the operations of addition and subtraction with signed numbers can be extended to the multiplication of these numbers by natural numbers, and

$$2 \times {}^-4 = {}^-8$$
$$2 \times {}^+4 = {}^+8$$

It is very important to note that, since multiplication has so far been seen as equivalent to repeated addition, there is as yet no meaning to be given to ⁻2×⁻4 or ⁺2×⁻4. This step is best deferred till the pupil is older, and able to use directed numbers with confidence within the limits so far explored. It needs a more complicated model than the simple one of left or right movement on a scale.

154

3 Fractions and rational numbers

Since all but the simplest fractions have ceased to be important in measurement and calculation, much of the traditional school work in fractions is no longer necessary. In actual use, the decimal fraction has replaced the vulgar fraction, and has been directly introduced in Chapter 3 as an extension of the base ten notation.

Nevertheless, the concept of a fraction and its recognition as a new kind of number is mathematically important. Fractions and the rules for operating with them extend the number concept still further. The concept itself is prior to mathematical treatment and arises from cutting or dividing whatever is taken as a whole. The child learns to ask for half a slice of bread long before he learns the symbol $\frac{1}{2}$. Moreover, the words half, quarter, third and eighth will remain in common use and survive all take-over by decimals in computation.

These words usefully form the starting point for an approach to fractions. Fraction strips made by folding serve to introduce the notation.

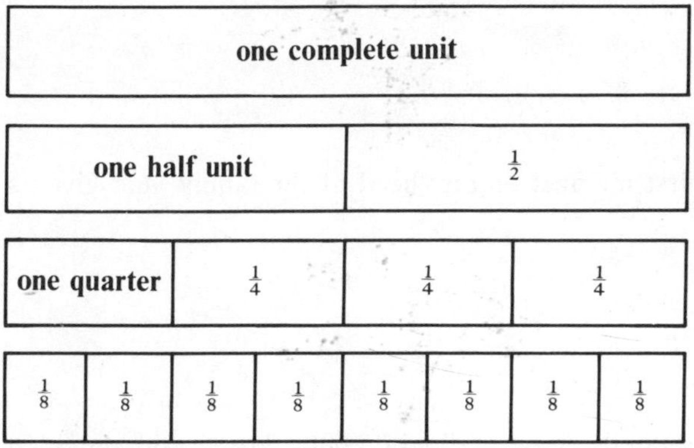

Figure 7.9

Fraction strips

The pupils themselves can make these strips and divide them up by folding. The word 'half', and its use for the strip folded in half is familiar, but the making of the strips and the formal development of quarters and eighths helps build up the concepts. Further notation should develop easily. One writes $\frac{1}{4}+\frac{1}{4}+\frac{1}{4}$ as $\frac{3}{4}$, the bottom number (denominator) indicating that the unit has been divided into four sub-units, and the top number (numerator) indicating that three of these are taken. The children should use these strips to answer such questions as "In how many ways can you write one whole unit?" "In how many ways can you write one half, or three-quarters?"

The concept of *equivalence* that emerges as they formulate

$$\frac{1}{2}=\frac{2}{4}=\frac{4}{8}$$
$$\frac{1}{1}=\frac{2}{2}=\frac{3}{3}$$

is an important one and forms the central concept from which the rules for addition and subtraction are developed.

The formal term 'equivalence class' (see page 176) is not used here. Instead, it is suggested that the equivalent fractions should be called a 'family'. This corresponds exactly to what a textbook may call 'an equivalence class of fractions'.

Thus the set

$$\{\tfrac{1}{2}, \tfrac{2}{4}, \tfrac{4}{8}, \tfrac{8}{16} \ldots\},$$

although its members are all different in the sense that the unit is divided differently, are the same in taking the same total amount from the unit, and may be called members of the same family.

Similarly, the members of the set $\{\tfrac{2}{3}, \tfrac{6}{9}, \tfrac{20}{30}\}$ are members of the same family, and such relations are conveniently shown on a number line suitably marked

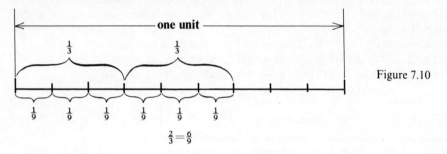

Figure 7.10

One can then take the first member as the 'head of the family' and give its name to the rest.

$$\{\tfrac{1}{2}, \tfrac{2}{4}, \tfrac{4}{8}, \tfrac{8}{16}\}$$

all belong to the $\tfrac{1}{2}$ family, while

$$\{\tfrac{2}{3}, \tfrac{6}{9}\}$$

belong to the $\tfrac{2}{3}$ family.

One could suggest that pupils draw a diagrammatic house and put in it members of fraction families. The exercise is no different from writing the members in brackets in set notation, but may help to make the association of the equivalent fractions more vivid.

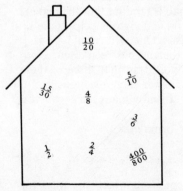

Figure 7.11

Some of the fraction family $\tfrac{1}{2}$

156

The word 'fraction' is associated with the division of concrete objects into parts, but in mathematics one wants to think of the ordered pairs in the form numerator/denominator as behaving like numbers, and they are usually called 'rational numbers', since the pair is written as a ratio. The fraction family then becomes a 'rational family', and one suggests that the term can be used in the primary school.

This enables one to describe as rational numbers the pairs shown on the two diagrams below.

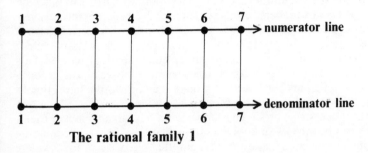

The rational family 1

Figure 7.12

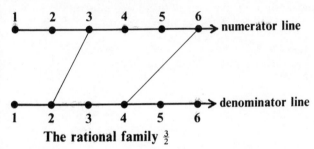

The rational family $\frac{3}{2}$

The first set of pairs gives a rational family, whose family name is the number 1, the second the 'mixed number' $1\frac{1}{2}$, formerly called an 'improper fraction'. The concept, 'rational number' unites all possible sets of pairs.

The number line diagrams, particularly if children are well used to them by the time they reach work with rationals, provide a clear mental picture of what is wanted. This diagram, for instance, illustrates a set of rational numbers whose denominator is 5.

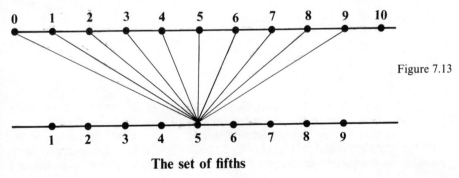

Figure 7.13

The set of fifths

157

Note that the word 'rational' now includes under one concept numbers such as $\frac{2}{5}$, 1, $1\frac{2}{5}$, 2.

A note is required about zero. Division by zero is excluded from arithmetical processes and hence the zero must be omitted from the denominator line. Division of zero by any number gives zero as the quotient, so that zero can be included in the set of rationals as a point on the numerator line. For primary work it is recommended that zero is included without comment, but without reference to possible zero denominators. It is often a sound teaching principle to avoid difficulties by not mentioning them! The number lines can also be extended to give directed numbers, but since division by negative integers has been omitted (see page 154) this cannot be done till secondary levels. The general concept of a signed rational is certainly beyond the reach of the primary child.

In a family, there is not only a family name, but individual names. This applies to the rational families. The fraction whose name is 'three ninths' belongs to the family 'one third'. This becomes not a mere play on words, but a breakthrough into the rules for adding and subtracting fractions.

The work with folded strips or single number lines has already shown that a fraction such as $\frac{3}{8}$ can be seen as an abbreviated form of $\frac{1}{8}+\frac{1}{8}+\frac{1}{8}$, corresponding to multiplication as continued addition. From this, it is seen that, where denominators are the same, addition is performed by adding numerators.

Here is the process set out in full for purposes of explanation

$$\frac{3}{9}=\frac{1}{9}+\frac{1}{9}+\frac{1}{9}$$
$$\frac{2}{9}=\frac{1}{9}+\frac{1}{9}$$
$$\frac{3}{9}+\frac{2}{9}= (\frac{1}{9}+\frac{1}{9}+\frac{1}{9})+(\frac{1}{9}+\frac{1}{9})$$
$$=\frac{5}{9}$$

One can now write immediately

$$\frac{3}{9}+\frac{2}{9}=\frac{5}{9}$$

If one needs the sum

$$\frac{1}{3}+\frac{2}{9}$$

the addition becomes one between the first members of two different families

$\frac{1}{3}$ belongs to $\{\frac{1}{3}, \frac{2}{6}, \frac{3}{9}, \frac{4}{12} \ldots\}$

$\frac{2}{9}$ belongs to $\{\frac{2}{9}, \frac{4}{18}, \frac{6}{27} \ldots\}$

But inspection shows that 'ninths' occur in both families, and these ninths can be added directly. One writes

$$\frac{1}{3}+\frac{2}{9}=\frac{3}{9}+\frac{2}{9}$$
$$=\frac{5}{9}$$

and similarly

$$\frac{2}{3}-\frac{1}{4}=\frac{8}{12}-\frac{3}{12}$$
$$=\frac{5}{12}$$

It is strongly recommended that all work in addition and subtraction of fractions should be done in this extended form, and that examples should be restricted to simple fractions that could appear in practical use, those whose denominators are small multiples of 2, 3, 5, or 10, so that a common denominator can be obtained by inspection or trial. Numerically large denominators and rules for the initial determination of lowest common denominators are rarely necessary in practice, and need not be used in the primary school.

There are many other ways, apart from those already given, of representing fractions as part of a whole and of showing rational numbers as number pairs. Paper folding is restricted to halves, quarters and eighths, but the use of squared paper enables any fraction to be shown by shading. The paper can either be cut into strips, into rectangles, or in irregular shapes built up from squares as in the figure.

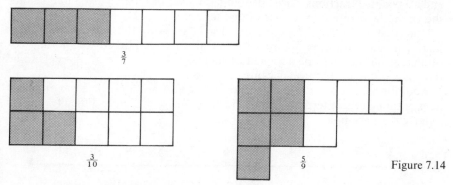

Figure 7.14

This activity ties up with work on area in a useful way.

A much more structured representation of rational numbers can be obtained from Cartesian co-ordinates (see Chapter 6) as in Figure 7.15. This is also more useful as a final class exercise in representing fractions since the work with co-ordinates relates to other topics in mathematics.

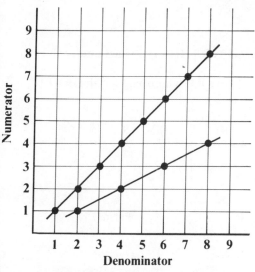

Figure 7.15

The rational families 1 and $\frac{1}{2}$

The vertical axis carries the numerator, the horizontal the denominator, and each fraction is represented by a dot, whose co-ordinates are these two numbers.

159

All points representing rationals belonging to the same family lie on straight lines, which can be drawn in lightly. The two lines shown link the families.

$$\{\tfrac{1}{1} \quad \tfrac{2}{2} \quad \tfrac{3}{3} \quad \ldots\}$$

and

$$\{\tfrac{1}{2} \quad \tfrac{2}{4} \quad \tfrac{3}{6} \quad \ldots\}$$

All rationals less than 1 are below the line bisecting the right angle, which itself represents the 1 family. Each point on the grid corresponds to a fraction, and all possible fractions whose denominators are less than a given number are shown on the diagram to the left of that number.

Note that in Figure 7.15 the vertical axis, carrying the numerator, is read first. This convention is opposed to that already established for plotting coordinates, but needs to be accepted as standard. In this context, it seems to be the obvious choice, but it may cause confusion.

Addition and subtraction of fractions may also be shown by using number lines, although the interpretation of the diagrams is now more difficult.

Here is an example.

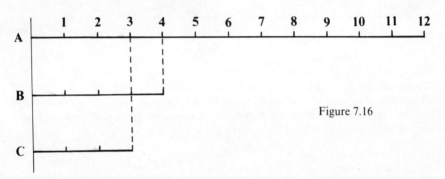

Figure 7.16

Taking line A as the unit, B is $\tfrac{1}{3}$ and C is $\tfrac{1}{4}$. If A is divided into twelve parts, one sees that $B = \tfrac{4}{12}$ and $C = \tfrac{3}{12}$ of A.

Drawing B and C end to end now gives a line whose length is the sum of B and C, or $\tfrac{7}{12}$ of A

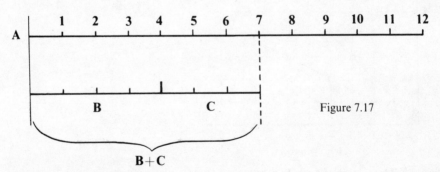

Figure 7.17

and the diagram represents

$$\tfrac{1}{3} + \tfrac{1}{4} = \tfrac{4}{12} + \tfrac{3}{12} = \tfrac{7}{12}$$

160

A similar diagram can be constructed for subtraction

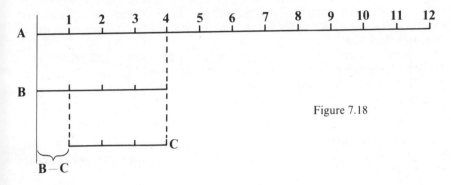

Figure 7.18

which represents

$$\tfrac{1}{3} - \tfrac{1}{4} = \tfrac{4}{12} - \tfrac{3}{12} = \tfrac{1}{12}$$

4 Decimal fractions

A decimal fraction differs from any other fraction only in the notation employed, which is developed from one introduced by Stevinius, a mathematician and engineer of the late sixteenth century. The work at the end of Chapter 3 has been done on the assumption that anyone who can add and subtract within the base ten place notation can also handle these operations with decimals.

The decimal system extends the notation for whole numbers by including place values which are fractions, and hence simple fractions need to be understood first. Early work with fractions can soon be made to include tenths, seen merely as a convenient sub-division along with halves and quarters.

Thus the pupil would be familiar with examples like

$$\tfrac{3}{10} + \tfrac{4}{10} = \tfrac{7}{10}$$
$$\tfrac{6}{10} - \tfrac{2}{10} = \tfrac{4}{10}$$

and treat these no differently from other fractional sums and differences. It is then pointed out that fractions in tenths are of wide and increasing practical use, so that a special way of writing them has been adopted, using a point to separate the tenths from whole numbers. Thus

$$1\tfrac{3}{10} \text{ becomes } 1\cdot3$$

The point appears as a *separator* and could be replaced by any other sign. In most European countries other than England, a comma is used. It is worth telling this to children, as it helps establish the conventional nature of the symbol.

If there is no whole number, a zero is usually written (and always written on the Continent) e.g.

$\tfrac{5}{10}$ is written $0\cdot5$.

161

This convention has no mathematical significance, but it draws attention to the existence of the point and the lack of a digit in the units column. Once the positional value of the decimal digits is set up, the zero helps avoid positional errors in column addition. This use of the zero is strongly recommended for *all* work with decimals.

The work at once links up with the notation for money and metric units where the point separates pounds from pence, or metres from centimetres. For both, the two digits following the separator are seen as hundredths

$$£1{\cdot}56 = £1\tfrac{56}{100}$$
$$2{\cdot}73 \text{ m} = 2\tfrac{73}{100} \text{ m}$$

It is now advisable to return to the abacus, to check place value for units, tens and hundreds and to extend to fractions, by columns to the right. The exchange values now run

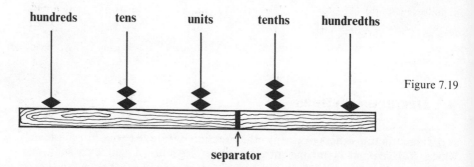

Figure 7.19

A dot or a coloured segment can be added to the abacus, which in the diagram is representing 122·31.

The situation is now formally in line with the earlier number work on the abacus.

It is probably worthwhile to show occasionally that the results from both the fractional and the decimal notation are the same. Using fractions

$$\tfrac{5}{10} + \tfrac{7}{10} = \tfrac{12}{10} = 1\tfrac{2}{10} = 1{\cdot}2$$

and with decimals

$$\begin{array}{r} 0{\cdot}5 \\ +\,0{\cdot}7 \\ \hline 1{\cdot}2 \end{array}$$

This can be done during the period when the transition between the notations is being made, but once this is made, it is better to continue with decimals without backward reference. Decimal fractions are a working notational device for handling sub-unitary quantities, and as such can be kept clear of alternative notations except when developing the topic.

A glance at almost any textbook of applied science or engineering shows that vulgar fractions have disappeared from practical computation. Modern currencies and metric measures can only conveniently be used with decimals, and for this reason decimal computation has been included in the number work of Chapter 3.

A note on 'places of decimals' is needed. This introduces concepts of accuracy and significance which are probably beyond the grasp of young children, but which are important as a background to their work.

Decimal calculation can proceed to any number of digits beyond the separating point. It is fairly easy to see that, if one can only measure to the nearest hundredth of a unit, computation to five places or more is meaningless.

An example will help show this. As a numerical calculation, one has the exact result

$$5 \cdot 23 \div 8 = 0 \cdot 65375.$$

If the $5 \cdot 23$ is the result of rounding off a measure in metres and millimetres to the nearest centimetre the original measure could lie anywhere between $5 \cdot 225$m and $5 \cdot 234$m, so that the quotient lies between $0 \cdot 653125$ and $0 \cdot 65425$ if worked as an exact decimal. One sees that only the first two figures are physically significant, hence one takes

$$5 \cdot 23 \text{ m} \div 8 = 0 \cdot 65 \text{ m}.$$

This discussion only becomes important for older students studying science or technology, but it needs raising at this point as a warning that practical computation can involve concepts requiring more mathematical maturity. The widespread use of calculators is now making this a matter for urgent consideration.

5   Ratio, proportion and percentage

Ratio and proportion
The concept of ratio entered mathematics in Greek geometry, when one line was measured in terms of another. One meets such expressions as 'AB is twice CD', which means that the measure of AB is 2 units if CD is the unit.

Various notations have been used, e.g.

  i $AB = 2CD$

  ii $CD = \frac{1}{2}AB$

  iii $CD:AB::1:2$

  iv $\dfrac{CD}{AB} = \dfrac{1}{2}$

  v $CD:AB = 1:2$

Of these **iv** is found most commonly in England, but **v** is the general form used in French or German schools. Our concept of a rational number comes from **iv**, and differs from that of a fraction in that it is not associated with a part of a whole. Mathematically, the symbol $\frac{1}{2}$ (as suggested on page 157) can be thought of merely as a numerator/denominator pair.

In practice, the use of the ratio as such is more important than the use of the fraction as such. Any two measures stand in a ratio to one another. This ratio is a number and not a measure.

Thus if AB=2 m, CD=1 m then

$$\frac{CD}{AB}=\frac{1}{2};$$

this is a number and is *not* $\frac{1}{2}$ m, which is a length.

Once again, the concept of equivalence classes, called 'families' in this chapter, is important.

If AB=4m and CD=2 m then

$$\frac{CD}{AB}=\frac{2}{4}$$

$$=\tfrac{1}{2}$$

and the 'family name' is used as before.

The quantities measured must be expressed in the same units.

If the mass of X is 5 g and that of Y is 6 kg, the ratio of their masses is not 5/6 but 5/6000.

The unit chosen does not matter; if it is milligrams then

$$\frac{\text{mass of X}}{\text{mass of Y}}=\frac{5000}{6\ 000\ 000}$$

$$=\tfrac{5}{6000}$$

using the family name as before.

The wide use of ratio in mathematics and its applications makes it a central concept, but at primary levels it is suggested that the work could stop at the expression of measures as ratios.

The concept of proportion is more difficult, and its formal use can be deferred. In the meantime, the relationship can be assumed. We say, of two distinct but related quantities, that *one is proportional to the other if a change in one produces a change in the other in the same ratio.* Thus the common-sense assumption that most children learn to make, that if one litre of water weighs a kilogram, then two litres will weigh two kilograms, is valid because mass and volume for a given liquid are proportional. This is an empirical result, but one is justified in taking it for granted at primary school level.

It is necessary for the junior child to realize when two quantities are *not* proportional. A square of cardboard of side 10 cm does not have twice the mass of a similar square of side 5 cm, and investigation with squares of card and a suitable balance soon shows this to be so. The reason only becomes clear when the pupil grasps the relation between lengths and areas. In this example, the mass is proportional to the area, and the result can readily be shown by marking the cardboard squares with a grid of unit squares.

Any examples less easily explained are best avoided at this stage.

Percentage

Reducing fractions to a common denominator in order to add them also enables them to be compared. It is, even with impracticably large denominators, easy to see at a glance that

$$\tfrac{376}{4321} \text{ is bigger than } \tfrac{371}{4321}$$

but it is not at once obvious which is the greater of $\frac{5}{6}$ and $\frac{7}{9}$. Using the equivalences $\frac{5}{6}=\frac{15}{18}$ and $\frac{7}{9}=\frac{14}{18}$ the comparison again becomes obvious.

It follows that all quantities expressible as ratios can conveniently be handled by using a fixed denominator, and this gives rise to the concept of percentage. A percentage is simply a ratio whose denominator is 100. Taken as a fraction, $\frac{3}{4}$ means that the unit is divided into 4 sub-units and 3 of them taken. This is equivalent to (belongs to the 'same family as') $\frac{75}{100}$, where there are 100 sub-units. Hence arises the expression 'per centum', early abbreviated to p/c and finishing as the familiar %.

Writing $\frac{3}{4}$ as 75% instead of $\frac{75}{100}$ is the only new feature. The essential concept is the choice of a fixed standard denominator.

Wherever quantities are compared with one another, work with percentage becomes one of the most common of all arithmetical processes. The need for use has, unfortunately, given rise to rules learnt by heart, such as the familiar 'to express one quantity as a percentage of another, write as a fraction and multiply by $\frac{100}{1}$'. These uses, however, lie in areas most of which are beyond the needs of primary children. Interest rates, discount, composition of alloys and compounds, growth rates, and so, although arithmetically straightforward, involve more mature knowledge and experience.

It is suggested therefore, that work at this level in primary schools should restrict itself to the simple concept of percentage, or to producing percentages as a special case of ratios.

Hence such activities as shading in or cutting out squares, as given on page 159, become exercises in understanding the term 'percentage', if the number of squares or other units is 100. It is only a matter of changing the notation. The seed box with its grid, as described in Chapter 6 to illustrate a co-ordinate system, gives the ratio

$$\frac{\text{number of seeds germinated}}{\text{number of seeds planted}}$$

directly as a percentage since 100 seeds are sown.

As a result of such activities, one would expect children to grasp the meaning of statements involving percentages, and to be aware of the percentage equivalents of common fractions, preferably establishing these by using sheets of squared paper.

6   The scale factor

One application of ratio deserves special discussion because it gives the lead into the rules for multiplication and division between fractional quantities. This is the concept of *scale*, which on a map, plan, model or drawing, is the ratio

$$\frac{\text{representational length or distance}}{\text{actual length or distance}}$$

Thus on a 1:50 000 map a distance of 1 cm represents 50 000 cm, or 2 cm represents 1 km. This ratio for maps is sometimes called the *representative fraction*, but the more general term is simply scale. Children usually become familiar with scale because of their interest in collecting accurate scale models as sold in toy shops. Catalogues of these commonly give full details of scale, usually in the notation $\times\frac{1}{n}$ where n is a convenient whole number. For maps and plans, there is now an international convention for agreed representative fractions.

Using centimetre or two centimetre squared paper, larger grids can be made by inking over the lines. With these it is a straightforward exercise to transform a simple outline drawing on one grid into a similar but enlarged shape on the other.

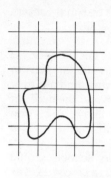
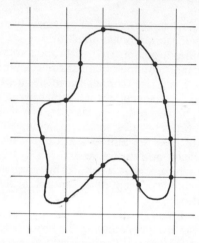

Figure 7.20

Consider first an outline whose dimensions are twice those of the original. Each distance in the original is multiplied by 2. Thus 6 cm becomes 2×6 cm $=$ 12 cm. By an already established convention this operation of doubling the scale is shown by the symbol $\times2$ rather than $2\times$. This should cause no difficulty and it has the advantage that $\times2$ is reserved for scale operations while $2\times$ continues to be understood as 'two lots of . . .' in multiplication. The expression $\times2$ is called the *scale factor*. In pictures of objects seen through a microscope it is often called the *magnification*. The word *enlargement* is also used.

In particular, one often needs a full size drawing or model, and then the scale is shown as $\times1$. This notation is important and needs to be stressed.

The next step is *reduction* in scale. To make a quarter size model one divides every dimension by 4, so that a length of say 24 cm becomes $\frac{24}{4}$ cm $=6$ cm.

One can also increase a scale and then reduce it by a different amount. If 24 is increased by a scale factor $\times3$ and then reduced to a quarter, it becomes

$$\frac{24\times3}{4}$$

Instead of writing it like this, the scale operators are put together and one writes

$$24\times\tfrac{3}{4}$$

The fraction then becomes a scale factor in its own right and is written as $\times\frac{3}{4}$.

Asked to compute a dimension to scale $\frac{3}{4}$, one multiplies by 3 and divides by four, but just as $\times2$ is equivalent to multiplication by 2, $\times\frac{3}{4}$ can be taken as multiplication by $\frac{3}{4}$. A practical rule for multiplying by a fraction emerges. Since the meaning of $\times1$ has already been stressed, $\frac{24}{4}$ can be written as $\frac{24\times1}{4}$ or, as before, $24\times\frac{1}{4}$. This suggests that multiplication by $\frac{1}{4}$ is equivalent to division by 4.

166

Children can now copy diagrams on scales such as $\times\frac{1}{2}$, $\times\frac{5}{2}$, $\times 3$, $\times 1$, if, but only if, the dimensions are chosen by the teacher to allow ready measurement and computation.

Although scale operations are usually done on measures, the actual arithmetic as always is one on the numbers, not the measures. It therefore makes sense to speak of operating on *numbers* with fractions which behave as scale factors. It is not necessary for the result to be a whole number. Thus

$$10 \times \tfrac{2}{7} = \tfrac{10 \times 2}{7}$$
$$= \tfrac{20}{7}$$
$$= 2\tfrac{6}{7}.$$

Nor is it necessary for the original measure or number to be an integer. For example

$$\tfrac{3}{4} \times \tfrac{1}{5} = \tfrac{3 \times 1}{4 \times 5}$$
$$= \tfrac{3}{20}$$

and one can now see why multiplication by fractions is done by multiplying numerators and denominators.

For some pupils, it might be better to introduce, as an intermediate stage, a fractional measure with an integral scale factor. Thus

$$\tfrac{2}{3} \times 4 = \tfrac{2 \times 4}{3}$$
$$= \tfrac{8}{3}$$

It is also possible to discuss multiplication by a decimal using the scale factor as an intermediate step

$$13 \times 0\cdot 3 = 13 \times \tfrac{3}{10}$$
$$= (13 \times 3) \div 10$$
$$= 39 \div 10$$
$$= 3\tfrac{9}{10}$$
$$= 3\cdot 9$$

which may then be compared with the direct process.

As with the subtraction of fractions, it is possible to show multiplication as a number line representation, again with the important proviso that its construction is more difficult than the arithmetical operation, and serves only to give the able child further insight. Here is

$$\tfrac{2}{3} \times 4 = \tfrac{8}{3}$$

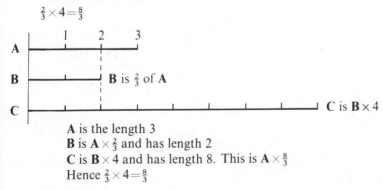

A is the length 3
B is $A \times \tfrac{2}{3}$ and has length 2
C is $B \times 4$ and has length 8. This is $A \times \tfrac{8}{3}$
Hence $\tfrac{2}{3} \times 4 = \tfrac{8}{3}$

Figure 7.21

167

The approach to multiplication through the scale factor gives a corresponding description of division through the *inverse scale factor*.

An inverse scale factor, applied to a scale drawing, transforms it back to its original size. For example, to produce a drawing on a scale $\times 3$ each dimension is multiplied by 3. Hence each dimension on the final drawing must be divided by 3 to return to the original, and it can be seen that the inverse of $\times 3$ is $\times \frac{1}{3}$.

Similarly the inverse of $\times \frac{1}{3}$ is $\times 3$.

Since a scale factor of $\times \frac{3}{4}$ means that each dimension has first been multiplied by 3 and then divided by 4, its inverse multiplies by 4 to reverse the original division, and divides by 3 to reverse the original multiplication. The inverse of $\times \frac{3}{4}$ is thus $\times \frac{4}{3}$.

Since one also calls the operation $\times \frac{3}{4}$ multiplication by a fraction, the inverse operation can be called division by a fraction since division is the inverse of multiplication. (See Chapter 2.)

Hence $8 \div \frac{3}{4}$ is the same as $8 \times \frac{4}{3}$.

Taken with the work of page 167 one sees finally that, for example

$$\frac{2}{3} \div \frac{5}{9} = \frac{2}{3} \times \frac{9}{5}$$
$$= \frac{18}{15}$$
$$= \frac{6}{5}$$
$$= 1\frac{1}{5}$$

It is not recommended that children do extensive work in the multiplication and division of fractions, but if the steps given are taken slowly with each stage linked with activities involving scale drawing, they should be able to use simple fractions with confidence. Without the parallel work with plans and drawings, the verbal explanations are difficult to follow, however carefully expressed. The use of the inverse scale factor may well be postponed till secondary levels, or, if used, not necessarily linked with division by fractions.

7　Modular arithmetic

Although numbers begin with the counting process, constructions such as the rationals count as numbers because they follow the same rules and can be operated on in the same way. A number system is one that forms addition and multiplication tables, subject to certain rules discussed in the next chapter.

A less well-known system is that of *modular numbers*. These can arise in considering the arithmetic of clocks and calendars, and are of value in the classroom in developing insight into number structure.

They arise if one tries to represent numbers on a circle instead of a straight line – on a clock face, that is, instead of a track, counting hours instead of centimetres.

A number line is indefinitely long, restricted only by the space available. The numbers and the points marking them increase without limit.

Now consider representation on a circle, as on the face of a clock. Take a four-hour timer, for simplicity, instead of a 12- or 24-hour dial.

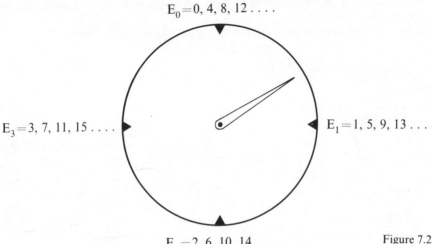

$E_0 = 0, 4, 8, 12 \ldots .$

$E_3 = 3, 7, 11, 15 \ldots .$

$E_1 = 1, 5, 9, 13 \ldots .$

$E_2 = 2, 6, 10, 14 \ldots .$

Figure 7.22

Here, the same four points serve to mark out the infinite sequence of hours or numbers. The set of numbers $\{0, 4, 8, 12 \ldots\}$ are all marked by the same point, and are in this sense *equivalent*. They form, like the set of numbers $\{\frac{1}{2}, \frac{2}{4}, \frac{3}{6}, \frac{4}{8} \ldots\}$ already discussed, an equivalence class.

The device has, in fact, divided the set of natural numbers into four distinct sets, which can be generated indefinitely by continuing round the circle. One can label the four sets by the symbols E_0, E_1, E_2, E_3, using as suffix the first number of each set. Arithmetically, what the members of each set have in common is that they give the same remainder when divided by four – the number of distinct points marked on the circle.

E_0 has the remainder 0

E_1 has the remainder 1

E_2 has the remainder 2

E_3 has the remainder 3

As the members of each class coincide with one another on the circumference, they are said to be *congruent*. This is written, using the symbol found in books on geometry

$5 \equiv 9$

This congruence, however, depends on the choice of *four* points. With 10 points the families would be different, so to keep everything clear, the relationship is written

$5 \equiv 9 \bmod 4$

and read: *5 is congruent with 9 modulo 4*. This apparently abstract statement becomes perfectly clear if the 'clock' face is consulted.

169

The smallest number in each class is often called the *residue*, and one can see that the residues for 4 are 0, 1, 2, 3. For 5 they would be 0, 1, 2, 3, 4, and so on. They are, of course, the remainders on division by the modulo number.

The behaviour of congruences can be investigated under the processes of addition and multiplication.

If, in ordinary arithmetic, any numbers a, b, c, d, are taken, and

$$a=b$$
$$c=d$$

then

$$a+c=b+d$$
$$ac=bd$$

This can easily be checked using any chosen numbers for a, b, c, or d. This is also true for the congruences (with residues shown in parentheses)

$$5\equiv9 \bmod 4\ (r=1)$$
$$15\equiv3 \bmod 4\ (r=3)$$

Adding, one gets

$$20\equiv12 \bmod 4\ (r=0)$$

and multiplying

$$75\equiv27 \bmod 4\ (r=3)$$

That is, the sums and products are also congruent, although with different residues.

Since each residue is congruent with itself, there is complete arithmetic of congruences modulo 4 whose only numbers are 0, 1, 2, 3. They obey the rules of ordinary numbers and one can make up addition and multiplication tables for them.

+	0	1	2	3
0	0	1	2	3
1	1	2	3	0
2	2	3	0	1
3	3	0	1	2

×	0	1	2	3
0	0	0	0	0
1	0	1	2	3
2	0	2	0	2
3	0	3	2	1

Each entry is, of course, obtained by adding or multiplying two members of the set of residues, dividing by 4 and recording the remainder in the table.

Those with an interest in the properties of numbers will find later that modular arithmetic is the key to much advanced work in this branch of mathematics. The results of modular arithmetic, although not normally discussed in technical terms, are of daily familiarity since all measurement of time, apart from the recording of years, uses a modulus. It is 12 or 24 for the hour of the day, 7 for the day of the week, 365 for the day of the year. To ask the question on what day Christmas fell in 1862 is to set a problem in arithmetic, modulo 7. Now that the 24-hour system has replaced the 12-hour day for rail time-tables, one sees that the larger the modulus the longer one goes on before meeting the residue. This is one of the justifications for the 24-hour clock, since each residue occurs once only in each day, instead of twice.

Arithmetical exercises done with these modular residue numbers look odd, but children who enjoy number work are intrigued by the oddness.

Each modular residue system has only as many numbers as that chosen for the modulus. For mod 4, as already seen, the four numbers in the system are 0, 1, 2, 3. They form a finite set. Here the system stops. It differs from a number system to base 4. This allows indefinite counting, using the symbols 0, 1, 2, 3 so that 'nine' is written 21 (as described in Chapter 2). Within the system modulo 4, 'nine' does not exist as such and is represented by 1, but this is only like saying the ninth day of the week does not exist, since one starts counting again after seven.

Examples of sums in modulo 4 would be

$$
\begin{array}{cccc}
2 & 2 & 2 & 1 \\
+3 & +2 & -1 & -2 \\
\hline
1 & 0 & 1 & 3 \\
\end{array}
$$

$3 \times 3 = 1$ $2 \times 3 = 2$

These can be done directly from the tables on page 70.

Subtractions can be done as inverses or directly by counting backwards. This can never land one on a number less than zero, so that the system does not require negative numbers.

Chapter 8

THE ALGEBRA OF SETS, RELATIONS AND NUMBERS

1 Introduction

The contents of this chapter are different in character from those of the preceding chapters, in which the concepts have been developed in relation to work with children in the classroom. In this chapter, the same ideas are put into a mathematical context and developed as background for the teacher. It is not a formal mathematical text, but a treatment of the underlying conceptual ideas intended to give the teacher insight into the reasons for the approaches described in previous chapters.

Although references are made to earlier chapters, material has been repeated where necessary for the sake of completeness. Apart from the section on punched cards and various examples which may prove useful in class, this chapter is not intended for use with children.

2 Sets and relations

The concept of a set is used in Chapter 2 and is defined as a collection which has two essential features.

  1 Its members are distinct from one another.

  2 There is a rule or criterion which enables one to decide whether or not a given entity belongs to the set.

Given a set, one can express relations between its members, and given two sets there may be relations between the members of each. Examples have already been discussed and represented in various ways, in particular by arrow diagrams as in Chapter 6, where their classroom uses are given.

172

Relations between sets

Relations between sets are often called *correspondences*, and one distinguishes four kinds. Consider the following sets, which children may have used:

A = {five children in a class}

B = {months of the year}

C = {soft drinks}

D = {numbers assigned to clothes pegs}

These sets may have been linked with arrows, each of which begins with a member of Set **A** and ends on a member of **B**, **C** or **D** as in the three figures.

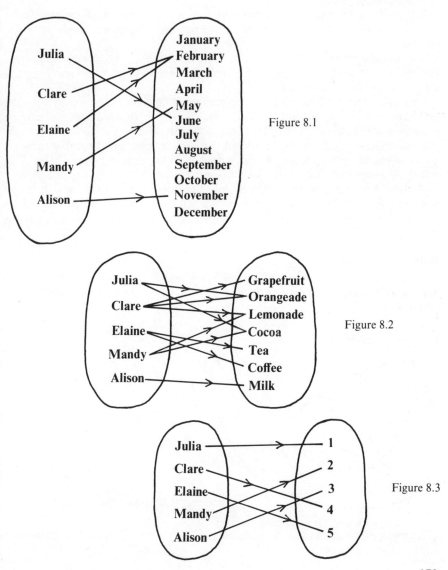

Figure 8.1

Figure 8.2

Figure 8.3

173

In Figure 8.1 the arrow reads, 'Has a birthday in . . .'.
In Figure 8.2 the arrow reads, 'Likes to drink . . .'.
In Figure 8.3 the arrow reads,'Hangs hats and coats on peg Number . . .'.

In Figure 8.1 there is only one arrow leaving each member of the first set (a child cannot have a birthday in more than one month), but more than one arrow can arrive at each member of the second set.

In Figure 8.2 there is more than one arrow leaving the members of the first set and more than one arrow arriving at members of the second set.

In Figure 8.3 there is *only one* arrow leaving each member of the first set and *only one* arrow arriving at each member of the second set. This relation is called one-one correspondence.

The reader will no doubt be able to think of a situation in which many arrows leave some members of the first set, but only one arrives at members of the second set.

Those relations as in Figure 8.1 and Figure 8.3 where there is only one arrow leaving every member of the first set, are called *functions* or *mappings*. They are used extensively in Chapter 6.

It is not suggested that the words function, one-one, etc. are used with the children, but it is important for them to realize that there is a difference between various relations between two sets. One of the first things a child has to learn is that, when he is counting, the relationship between objects and number names is a one to one correspondence. A very young child learning to count often chants numbers completely out of step with his movements as he sorts out the objects.

It should be realized that there is more to these arrow diagrams than just making pictures. The concept of function which is introduced through these pictures can help with other ideas of function and relation as they gradually develop.

Relations on a set

Where it is between members of a single set, a relation is said to be *on* the set. In Figure 8.4 the arrow reads, 'is greater than' and expresses such a relation on the set {3, 4, 5, 6, 7}.

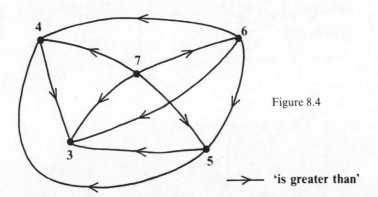

Figure 8.4

$\longrightarrow$— 'is greater than'

The use of arrows in this way enables us to classify relationships on a set in quite a rigorous way.

Consider the following:

1 The relation 'is less than' on the set {3, 5, 6, 7, 9, 11}.
2 The relation 'is a factor of' on the set {3, 5, 6, 7, 9, 11}.
3 The relation 'gives the same remainder as when divided by 4' on the set {3, 5, 6, 7, 9, 11}.

It would help the reader's understanding of this if he would draw the diagrams for himself, before looking at those that follow.

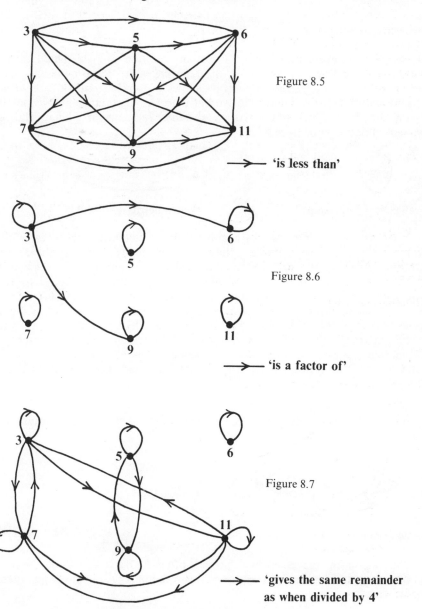

Figure 8.5

———➤— 'is less than'

Figure 8.6

———➤— 'is a factor of'

Figure 8.7

——➤ 'gives the same remainder
as when divided by 4'

175

One can see a number of differences here between the diagrams. These illustrate differences in the actual relationships. In Figure 8.5 it will be seen that for every two arrows there is always a third, i.e. if a—→—b and b—→—c then a—→—c. This kind of relationship is called *transitive*, because it passes over directly from a to c.

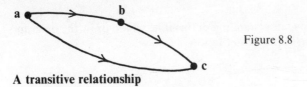

Figure 8.8

A transitive relationship

In Figure 8.6, every number is a factor of itself, i.e. a—→—a. This kind of relationship is called *reflexive*, as in the reflexive verb, 'I wash myself'. The diagram of a reflexive relationship always shows a loop. In Figure 8.7, the relationship is both transitive and reflexive but there are also return arrows, i.e. if a—→—b, then b—→—a, where the arrow is the *same* relationship. This is called a *symmetric* relationship.

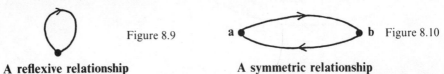

Figure 8.9   a   b   Figure 8.10

A reflexive relationship   **A symmetric relationship**

A relationship which is always transitive, reflexive and symmetric is called an *equivalence relation*. An example is the relation normally shown by the equals sign, but it is important to realize the different ways in which we use the words equivalent or same. Things can be called the same or equivalent if they have the same colour or shape or, indeed, any shared characteristic. Any one member of a set of equivalent entities can be chosen as a *representative* of the set. Thus, if one wishes to demonstrate the colour 'red' in a language lesson, any red object will do; all objects that have the characteristic 'red' are equivalent or the same for this purpose (see also the use of the word 'same' in Chapter 5).

In Chapter 7 the concept of equivalence has been made the basis of the treatment of fractions. The set

$$\{\tfrac{1}{2} \ \tfrac{2}{4} \ \tfrac{3}{6} \ \tfrac{4}{8} \ \tfrac{5}{10} \cdots \}$$

has on it a relation of numerical equality whose arrows show it to be transitive, reflexive and symmetric.

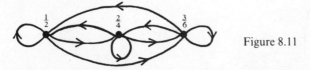

Figure 8.11

An equivalence relation

From this set the representative chosen is often the fraction with the smallest denominator. In Chapter 7, the name of this fraction serves as the family name of the set.

176

It is not necessary for children to be able to classify relations in this way, but they should certainly know that there are different kinds and if they explore them using arrow diagrams they will realize this.

It will be seen that the relation, 'is equal to' is in fact rather complicated, and, therefore, we need not be afraid to introduce kinds of relation other than equality to children. One of the commonest relations met by children is the *ordering* relation, so called because it places the members of a set in order. An example is given in Figure 8.4. If a relation for all members of the set is not symmetric or reflexive but is transitive, it is an ordering relation for the set.

Figure 8.12

Children ordered by relation 'is taller than'
(see also fig 8.4)

Children meet a great many ordering relations such as 'is lighter than', 'is heavier than', 'is shorter than', 'is longer than', and so on, and they should certainly meet along with these the ordering relations on number – 'is less than' symbolized as $<$, and 'is greater than', written as $>$. Chapter 2 suggests introducing these symbols at the same time as the equals sign.

The actual operation of putting in order is a fundamental activity prior to all mathematics. It is important to note that many orderings associated with measure can in fact be done directly. One can arrange children in order of size without finding their heights. Nevertheless, numerical ordering, like alphabetical ordering, is often used in practice, and children can profit by the exercise of arranging a set of numbers in order, using the relation 'is less than' or 'is greater than'.

Sequences of numbers such as

$$\frac{1}{2} \quad \frac{1}{4} \quad \frac{1}{8} \quad \frac{1}{16} \quad \frac{1}{32}$$

or

$$1 \quad 3 \quad 5 \quad 7 \quad 9 \quad 11$$

usually arise in one of these orderings.

The relation which performs the reverse process is called the inverse relation; e.g. 'is the father of' is the inverse of 'is the son of' on a set of males; 'is half of' is the inverse of 'is the double of' on a set of numbers. This concept of inverse will be developed later.

177

3   Operations on sets

As well as the relations between sets and the relations between the members of a set, one can consider means of combining sets.

One of the most important ideas is one of the simplest.

A sub-set of a set is simply a set taken from another one. For example {a, b, c, d, e, f, g} has a very large number of sub-sets, some of which are {a, b}, {a}, {c, d, e, f}, {a, g}, etc. If A = {a, b, c, d, e, f} and B = {a, b}, then we say that B is a 'sub-set of' or 'included in' A and write B ⊂ A. If a set is divided up into sub-sets that have no common members, but which between them contain all the members of the set, it is said to be *partitioned*. For example, {a, b, c, d} and {e, f, g} is one of the possible partitions of {a, b, c, d, e, f, g}.

Another useful technical term is 'universe'. In ordinary use this means 'all that exists', but in mathematics it is given the special meaning of 'all that we are concerned with'. Thus, if one is discussing which numbers are prime, the universe is the set of whole numbers. If one is deciding which set of children stay to school dinner, the 'universe' is the whole class. Other terms are 'universal set' and 'universe of discourse'.

If one takes as a universe a pack of cards, there are many possible sub-sets; hearts, clubs, red cards, black cards, threes, fours, picture cards, etc. Notice that some of these sets are included in others and some of the sets have common members.

Consider the set of cards making up the hearts, and the set of threes. If arranged as in the figure

Figure 8.13

one sees that there is one member common to both sets. The set formed by this card is called the *intersection* of the two sets.

178

As another example, the intersection of the set of picture cards and the set of red cards consist of the cards the two sets have in common, that is

Figure 8.14

The notation for intersection is ∩, best read as 'intersection'. So that one could write, for Figure 8.13

{Hearts} ∩ {Threes}={Three of hearts}.

To take another example:

If A={a, b, c, d, e}, B={a, e, i, o, u}.
Then A ∩ B={a, e}.

The other way in which one can combine sets is to put two together, and this is called *union*. By putting together the hearts and the threes one gets all the hearts together with the three of clubs, diamonds and spades. Notice that the three of hearts only appears once although it is in both sets since a set does not allow repetition. The symbol for union is ∪ so that the set formed by the union of A={a, b, c} and B={d, e, f} is written

A ∪ B and is the set {a, b, c, d, e, f}.

Forming the union of two sets is the opposite procedure to forming sub-sets from a set. If the two sets have no common members the separation of these sets from the union would be a partitioning of the set. This is not true if they have members in common.

It is possible to make pictures of these operations of sets, but it is very necessary to warn that, as with all diagrams, it is dangerous to draw conclusions unless one can be certain that the diagram represents all possible cases.

Diagrams of sets are usually called Venn diagrams, after the English logician John Venn. Venn's original diagrams were different from the ones now most commonly used, and were devised for a different purpose. On these diagrams one draws the outline of a region as a loop and considers the members of the set to be within the region, e.g.

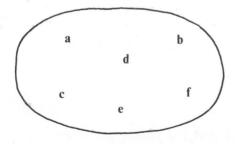

Figure 8.15

The outline has been drawn as a free-hand loop to emphasize that it does not matter at all what shape the boundary is; the drawing is purely diagrammatic.

The universe can be represented as a rectangle enclosing the loops. Although this is often left out when there is no fear of ambiguity, in the early stages of work with sets it is important to be clear about what universe is under discussion.

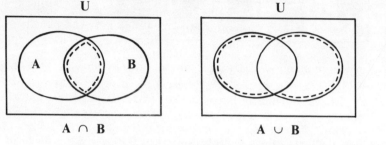

Figure 8.16

$A \cap B$ $A \cup B$

The universal set, intersection and union

The sets $A \cap B$ and $A \cup B$ have been outlined to show the region containing the members of these sets. To shade in these regions could lead to confusion with ideas of area and is not done here, although shaded diagrams are commonly seen.

The next figure shows set inclusion; $A \subset B$ is a statement about two sets and is not an operation giving rise to a third set.

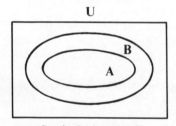

Figure 8.17

Set inclusion $A \subset B$

An example will show some of these ideas more clearly. If the universe is taken as the numbers 1 to 21; A the set of multiples of 2, and B the set of multiples of 3, one can represent them on a diagram.

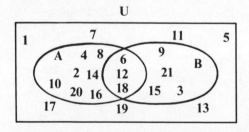

Figure 8.18

It is clearly seen from this diagram that, if M_2 is written for the set of multiples of 2, M_3 for the set of multiples of 3, etc., then

$$M_2 \cap M_3 = M_6$$

180

4   Two-way systems

As pointed out at the beginning, one of the most important characteristics of a set is that something is either a member of a set or not. It must be a quite clear-cut two-way decision. In order to be able to define the sub-set of blue-eyed children in a set of children in a classroom, one would first have to agree about what were 'blue eyes' – a task that might prove extremely difficult in practice. But without this agreement the set cannot be defined.

The set, in fact, links up with what logicians call 'two-term logic' – the discussion of questions where there can be a clear-cut decision, an unambiguous yes or no. Many physical situations model this two-term logic. A switch controlling a light is either on or off, or a position on a paper tape is either punched with a hole or it is not. These physical situations are called, 'two-state systems'.

A very useful two-state system consists of cards with a row of holes punched along one edge and (usually) numbered for reference. Each hole can either be left as it is or made into a slot by cutting out the card.

This card now becomes a useful way of storing information about set membership, and it is quite easy for top junior pupils to use.

The example given uses only four holes, but in practice up to ten holes can be used quite conveniently.

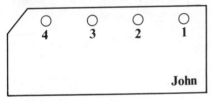

Figure 8.19

Each child can have his own card with his name on it and the four holes can represent information about the child. For example

   1 Are you a boy?
   2 Do you own a pet?
   3 Do you own a bicycle?
   4 Do you live in a bungalow?

In the example, these are given as Yes/No questions and each child cuts a slot if he is a member of that particular set. This gives us a limited amount of information. A slot cut in position 4 will tell us that that child lives in a bungalow, but a hole in position 4 merely tells us the child does *not* live in a bungalow; it does not tell us what kind of place he does live in. Note, however, that if no slot is cut in position 1, the child must be a girl, since boy/girl is itself a two-state system.

If Frances lives in a bungalow and has a pet but no bicycle her card will be

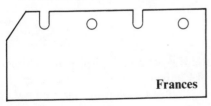

Figure 8.20

(One of the corners is best cut off so that one can tell quickly which way round the cards should be.)

If each child makes a card like this, one can quickly sort out the various members of the different sets by putting all the cards together in a pack and placing a knitting needle or some other kind of rod through the required hole. If one places a rod through hole 3, for instance, and shakes the cards, those belonging to the children who own bicycles will all drop off.

To find those who own a bicycle *and* own a pet, one can put a rod through hole 2 and shake. This gives the pet owners. Put these cards shaken off together again, and pass the rod through hole 3 and shake. Those that drop off own both pets and bicycles.

If A is the set of bicycle owners and B is the set of pet owners, this procedure has given the intersection of A and B, or $A \cap B$.

Now put a rod through hole 3 in the cards remaining and give another shake. This will give the bicycle owners who are not pet owners. The three lots of cards that have been shaken off put together give the set of those who own a bicycle *or* own a pet. This set is the union of A and B, $A \cup B$. Note that the union is equivalent to the inclusive 'or', not the disjunctive. It is really and/or. The disjunctive 'or' (either/or but not both) gives a set combination not considered here.

It is not suggested that punched cards should be used as a means of teaching sets, but they do form a way of sorting and recording information useful in practice and which children enjoy. Once children have understood the principles, they will almost certainly devise for themselves interesting things to do with the cards.

The hole/slot is in fact a binary code. The hole corresponds to 'no', the slot to 'yes', or, using a numerical code,

hole $= 0$

slot $= 1$.

Each child's data can be represented as a four-digit binary number, corresponding to the holes and slots. Thus Frances, whose card is shown in Figure 8.18, is coded as 1010, and this at once shows her set membership.

N.B. It may be found that some accounts of punched cards use the coding

hole $= 1$

slot $= 0$.

Logically this makes no difference as long as it is clear which code is used. The advantage of the slot $= 1$ is that the child cuts it if he is a member of the set. To cut the slot for a negative statement seems less natural.

5 The structure of number systems

The actual number systems whose study and use form part of primary mathematics have been discussed in some detail in Chapters 2, 3 and 7. The object of this section is to set out the structure of *any* number system, to lay down the rules that must be obeyed by a set of entities before they can qualify to count as numbers.

It is very difficult indeed to get the feel of these laws. They are easily understood, but at first glance seem merely to clothe the obvious in devious technical language. In fact, they have been abstracted from general experience in working with numbers and doing arithmetic. It is certainly not suggested that children should be taught these laws, the effort would be misplaced and possibly harmful.

The laws are quite independent of positional notation and column exchange values, but like them govern the forms of computation actually used. Their formulation is most readily done by considering the set of natural numbers

$$\{1, 2, 3, 4, 5, 6, \ldots\}$$

with the exclusion of zero.

On this set there are two fundamental binary operations, that is, operations involving pairs of numbers. These are addition and multiplication. Although for natural numbers multiplication may be thought of as continued addition, it is certainly not so for fractions, and so it will be logged as a distinct operation.

Now when addition or multiplication is performed with any number pair, the result is always another natural number. This property of keeping the result of an operation within the set is called *closure* and gives the first of the formal laws for natural numbers.

1 The set is closed to addition and multiplication. If a and b are numbers, so are

$$a+b$$

$$a \times b$$

It is also true that the order of the pair is immaterial; the operation is commutative. This gives a second law.

2 Within the set addition and multiplication are commutative:

$$a+b=b+a$$

$$a \times b = b \times a$$

If more than two numbers are involved, the operations are still done in pairs, but one has alternative routes to the final result, for example

$$2+3+4=5+4$$
$$=9$$

or

$$2+3+4=2+7$$
$$=9$$

Each intermediate route has been produced by associating the numbers in different pairs. Using a bracket notation this can be written as

$$(2+3)+4=2+(3+4)$$

and hence one arrives at the third law.

3 Within the set addition and multiplication are associative.

$$(a+b)+c=a+(b+c)$$

$$(a \times b) \times c = a \times (b \times c)$$

The next formulation, important and already used in devising an algorithm for long multiplication, can be shown by a preliminary example.

$$2 \times (4+3) = (2 \times 4) + (2 \times 3)$$
$$= 8 + 6$$
$$= 14$$

The multiplier 2 has operated on both the 4 and the 3 within the brackets. This gives the fourth formal law.

4 Within the set the operation multiplication is distributive over addition

$$a \times (b+c) = (a \times b) + (a \times c)$$

or, as usually written

$$a(b+c) = ab + ac$$

Note that the reverse is *not* true: addition does not distribute over multiplication.

$$a + (b \times c) \neq (a+b) \times (a+c)$$

These four laws have been obtained by examining arithmetical operations on the natural numbers. Using the modified operations that extend addition and multiplication to fractions, it is easily seen that fractions also obey them. It is also true for directed numbers; although Chapter 7 expressly excludes as a primary topic multiplication of these by one another. This now leads to a general abstract definition of a number system.

A number system is any set of entities which can be combined in pairs by each of two processes called addition and multiplication, which obey the four laws set out above.

Note particularly that the properties of subtraction and division do not form part of the formulation. One sees that

$$a \div b \neq b \div a$$
$$(4-2) - 1 \neq 4 - (2-1)$$

so that laws 2 and 3 do not hold for these processes.

The systems of directed numbers and rationals differ from the set of natural numbers in one further respect. They are said to form *extended* number systems. Briefly, these are sets of numbers closed to more operations than addition and multiplication. Consider, for example, division. Twelve pennies can be shared equally among six children, but not among seven. Hence our natural number system, keeping in step as it does with collections of real objects, allows $12 \div 6$ but not $12 \div 7$. The system is not closed to division, but many pairs are excluded. But the system of fractions or rationals allows such pairs. Applied to situations where sub-division is physically possible, the fraction gives a useful numerical result. Within this system $12 \div 7 = \frac{12}{7}$ or $1\frac{5}{7}$, and it is, therefore, closed to division as well as addition and multiplication.

The entire situation can be seen by asking what goes in the box if the following seven statements are to be true. Where the box symbol is repeated, the *same* number goes in each.

1. $5 - \square = 3$
2. $5 - \square = 8$
3. $5 \times \square = 10$
4. $5 \times \square = 9$
5. $\square \times \square = 4$
6. $\square \times \square = 2$
7. $\square \times \square + 2 = 0$

The natural number system fits the boxes for **1**, **3** and **5** but offers nothing available that fits the others. The extended number systems enable one to fill more and more of the boxes. Statement **4** is completed by the use of the rational number system mentioned above, **2** by a member of the set of signed integers, namely $^-3$ or negative 3. Statements **6** and **7** remain incomplete within the systems discussed in this book, although **6** is completed by real numbers and **7** by complex numbers. The nature of these two can be left as an open question for any reader interested in following it. The modular numbers also discussed in Chapter 7 are interesting in that they do not form an extended system since they are already closed to the operations of $+$, $\times$. They do, however, form a finite number system. For example, the integers (mod 4) are $\{0, 1, 2, 3\}$

$$2 + 3 \equiv 1 \ (\text{mod } 4)$$
$$2 \times 3 \equiv 2 \ (\text{mod } 4)$$

Each extended number system is complete in its own right, containing numbers which have all the properties of simpler systems as well as the enriched properties. Thus the system of signed integers contains $^+4$ which does all the things that 4 does. We say that $^+4$, which belongs to the set of all signed integers, *corresponds to* 4, which belongs to the set of natural numbers. It is not, however, identical with it, having properties of its own that 4 lacks. For example, 4 has the square root 2, shown diagrammatically by the side of a square whose area is four units, but $^+4$ has *two* square roots $^+2$ and $^-2$.

6 Identities, inverses and algebras

Identities

The concept of 'identity' or 'identity element' is found in all mathematical operations on sets, whether these are of numbers, spatial elements or more abstract structures. Children will meet this concept in many different situations, although for them it will be implied rather than explicitly formulated.

Consider as examples a few sets and appropriate operations.

1 The set of whole numbers and addition.

2 The set of possible indications of the hour-hand of a clock with a 12-hour dial when on the hour, and the operation of moving the hands a given number of hours.

3 The set of rotational symmetries of a rectangle as discussed in Chapter 5, with the operation 'followed by'.

4 The set of natural numbers and multiplication.

In each of these sets there is a member which, when used according to the operation, leaves the situation unchanged. This member or element is called the identity. Thus, if zero is added to 2, the number is unchanged. For any number n,

$$n+0=n$$

so that 0 is the identity for addition within the natural number system. It is also the identity for subtraction, since

$$n-0=n$$

For the 12-hour clock, the identity is 12 hours. If the hour-hand is advanced 12 hours, its reading is unchanged. It is true that the physical situation is not the same and that the hour-hand has now made one complete revolution, but its actual indication is unchanged provided that the clock has a 12-hour dial.

If $t=$ time in hours

$$t+12=t$$

This is an example from the modular arithmetic of Chapter 7. In the notation given there one could write

$$(3+12)\equiv3 \ (\text{mod } 12)$$

For the rotational symmetry positions of the rectangle there are only two possibilities, repeated here for reference.

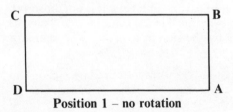

Position 1 – no rotation

Figure 8.21

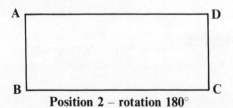

Position 2 – rotation 180°

There is the original unrotated position, and rotation through 180°. Since the operation was one rotation 'followed by' another, rotation 180° 'followed by' rotation $0°$ leaves the rectangle at rotation $180°$. Once again, the zero rotation corresponds to leaving the situation unchanged and is the identity for this set of two positions.

Finally, the identity for the multiplication of natural numbers is clearly 1

$$1 \times n = n$$

and this is also the identity for division.

The child learning the operations of arithmetic has to learn to handle the identities for each operation with confidence. The child does not need to use the term, but the teacher should find it a help in discussion if he himself is familiar with the concept over a wide range of use.

Inverses

The equally important concept of inverse, used in Chapter 7 in discussing the inverse scale factor, can now be defined.

Given a set and an operation on it, the inverse of any member (or element) is the element which combined with it, gives the identity.

Taking the four sets given on page 186

1 There is no inverse for any member. There is no natural number which added to another gives zero.

2 Each hour position has an inverse. 12 is self inverse, and for all other times the inverse is $(12-t)$.

3 Each element is self inverse.

4 There are no inverses except for 1, which is self inverse.

These examples make it clear that the concept of inverse is more complex than that of identity. Examination of the extended number systems shows that they do possess inverses not found in the set of natural number. The set of signed integers possesses additive inverses, since, for example

$$^+3 + {^-3} = 0$$

The set of rationals possesses multiplicative inverses

$$\tfrac{3}{2} \times \tfrac{2}{3} = 1$$

The set of signed rationals possesses both.

Note that the 'traditional' account of fractions discusses a 'cancelling' operation. This is a mis-statement of what actually occurs, because in fact one is using identity operations.

Teachers will be familiar with the howler

$$\tfrac{2}{3} \times \tfrac{3}{2} = 0$$

where the language of 'cancelling' has lead to an incorrect analogy with $3-3=0$.

If the concept of inverse operations can be made clear by implication, pupils should have less difficulty in operating with fractions and negative numbers.

Algebras

The word algebra still carries the idea of arithmetic done with letters which stand for numbers. As mathematics has developed over the past century, the idea of an algebra has developed along with that of a number system. This chapter has tried to show that arithmetic depends on general rules which enable one to decide what can or cannot be done.

Systems which obey such general rules are called algebras; there is not only the algebra of numbers, but the algebra of more general sets. Behind everything is the quite fundamental concept of a pair of elements from a set and an operation combining them.

Given the set and the operation one can ask four questions.

1 Is there an identity element?

2 Is there an inverse element?

3 Is it commutative?

4 Is it associative?

If there are two possible operations in a set then one can also ask

5 Does the first distribute over the second?

6 Does the second distribute over the first?

These questions have already been answered for the arithmetical operations with numbers. But they are perfectly general questions that can be applied to any mathematical structure consisting of elements and the operations in them. Any one algebra does not need to obey all these laws, but in mathematics today one recognizes various kinds of algebra according to what laws are obeyed.

In the future many children are going to meet at the secondary stage all kinds of structures that obey some of these laws but not others. They are, in fact, going to work with many algebras. The importance of this to the primary school is that the possibility of systems that do not obey the rules of arithmetic should be kept open to the children; and that the children should come to realize what the important rules are. For the teacher, this suggests a much wider grasp of mathematical structure than was needed for the kind of things that the teacher learnt at school.

Chapter 9

PROBABILITY AND CHANCE

1 Probability as a primary school topic

The study of probability is a branch of mathematics having a wide range of applications, both technical and social. It is an admirable topic to introduce at primary level, not only because intelligent pupils will be able to apply its basic concepts as their thinking matures, but because it emerges from simple activities and calls at this level for very easy number work.

It is the possibility of organizing these activities and recording their results numerically and graphically, not merely as school exercises but extended to ideas outside the classroom, that makes them appeal to teachers. The developed concept of probability is a difficult one, and for the pupils must remain largely intuitive, but given understanding on the part of the teacher, its early stages are fairly easy for children to grasp. Once grasped, the implications for social training are notable, particularly in helping one to adopt a questioning attitude to advertising pressures and to general statements about the economy. The direct bearing of probability theory on modern statistical techniques, quality control procedures and the like is, of course, an advanced topic of study. Yet it is true that the simple ideas discussed in this chapter remain valid in more sophisticated contexts. They are also, without any further development, of value to the adult in his day to day judgements.

Only Sections 1, 5 and 6 of this chapter are of direct application in the classroom. Sections 2, 3 and 4 discuss the concept of probability as a background for the teacher. They may make difficult reading, as it is not easy to make probability into a precisely defined term, although the difficulties over the basic concepts only become apparent on mature discussion. For the pupil, the two aspects of probability outlined in the next two sections need not be fully separated. It is not even essential for the teacher, although the discussion gives more adult interest to a topic otherwise left as elementary.

2 Experimental probabilities

If a box of drawing pins is accidentally spilled, some of them land on their heads and some land point downwards. If a single pin from the box is dropped, one cannot say in advance which way it will drop, yet if the spillage of the boxful is repeated deliberately, a numerical result emerges. Counting shows that the ratios

number of pins point downwards
———————————————————————
total number of pins dropped

if calculated for each trial, are about the same, providing that there are sufficient pins and that they are dropped each time from the same height on to the same surface. Moreover, if the results for, say, ten trials are averaged out, the results for the next ten dropped under the same conditions are usually quite close.

There are many factors which will alter the value of the ratio. For example:

1 Different types or makes of drawing pin give consistently different results.

2 The ratios for each individual trial show much greater variation if the number of pins is small.

3 The results are very sensitive to changes of conditions. A hard plastic laminate surface gives different ratios from a thick blanket, and so do small changes in height or shaking movement as the pins are tipped.

4 On the other hand, there is an important conclusion that gives the topic its practical application. If the experiment is repeated a large number of times under constant conditions, the ratio settles down to a value that is itself substantially constant. This settling-down process is sometimes called the Law of Large Numbers for trials of this kind. It is also true that this settling-down process sometimes requires very large numbers indeed if the ratio is small.

This ratio is called the *occurrence ratio*. If the experiment is thought of as finding out how many pins will settle on their points, it can be named the *success ratio*. It is always obtained from observation and recording of what has actually happened. It can then be used to predict in advance the results of a future series of trials. There is, however, no logical guarantee that the occurrence ratio will follow, and in any case some trivial difference such as tipping the box less gently may affect the result. The occurrence ratio as determined for an experiment in the past is renamed a *probability* for an outcome as yet unsettled.

If none of the pins land on their points, the occurrence ratio is zero, but it cannot be negative. Similarly, if the pins all land on their points, the ratio would be unity, but it could not be greater than this. Hence all occurrence ratios lie between the extreme values 0 and 1. Clearly, an occurrence ratio of $\frac{1}{2}$ is equivalent to 50% success in the experiment. Using the language of mathematics, occurrence ratios, and hence probabilities based on them, are rational numbers lying between 0 and 1, written as

$$0 < p < 1$$

Now consider a numerical example.

Suppose 100 flat-headed drawing pins are dropped 10 times and a total of 637 fall on their points, then the occurrence or success ratio is

$$\frac{\text{number falling point down}}{\text{number dropped}} = \frac{637}{1000} \text{ or } 0.637$$

This is a record of what has happened and the result is not open to argument. It is then assumed that, if the trials are repeated, the results will be substantially the same, i.e. that the probable or expected value of the count of 'points down' will be 637 for 1000 dropped pins. (One would not be surprised however to get 631 or 652, or any number in the neighbourhood.) In the same way that manufacturers find it convenient to work with the unit cost of an item that can only be mass produced in thousands, mathematicians find it convenient to allot the probability to a single trial. One gets the statement:

The probability of a flat-headed drawing pin landing point down is 0·637.

This statement sometimes causes unnecessary difficulty. If a pin is actually dropped, it will fall either point up or point down, and one is presented with a simple fact. But the probability concept applies to results as yet undecided or unobserved. Assigned to a single event, it implies that some large multiplier is used, just as a unit cost of 0·013p implies that an article is being produced in batches.

The correct interpretation of the statement in bold type is an extended statement like this:

If the experiment of dropping a pin of this type in this way is repeated a large number of times, then the expected value of the occurrence ratio is 0·637. The expectation is based on the results of previous trials.

Once this is quite clear, there should be no difficulty with these quantified statements about single future events.

The example has been chosen because it is an experiment easily visualized and easily performed without special apparatus. The principles apply to all examples, however complicated. The following are taken from areas not normally dealt with in the primary school, but help to show the range of the concept.

1 It is well known that the atoms of some elements like radium break up spontaneously into fission products which include lighter atoms. An elaborate experimental procedure shows that of every gram of radium 0·5 g will have decayed in this way after about 1600 years. This means that half the atoms have then broken down, so that

$$\frac{\text{number of atoms decayed in 1600 years}}{\text{original number of atoms}} = \frac{1}{2}$$

For this reason, 1600 years is sometimes said to be the 'half-life' of the kind of radium atom in question. Applied to a single atom of radium, the concept of 'half-life' seems absurd; it may break up within the next second, or it may last a million years. No one knows until it has happened.

But the smallest visible sample of radium contains trillions of atoms – so many that the Law of Large Numbers comes into operation, and the ratio settles down to a value that can be taken as a natural physical constant, published in a list of the properties of radium.

2 If a man wishes to take out a 'whole life' policy, the insurance company obtains details of his age and medical condition and quotes him accordingly. In effect, by paying this premium, the man is betting on the probability of his dying young and leaving his family in want. The company bets him he will live! If he lives, he loses the bet and his premium helps keep the company going. If he dies, the company loses and their pay-out helps to support his family. How does the company ensure that it remains solvent? Firstly, by basing its demands for premiums on the mortality tables which record the death rates of

the various age groups in the community, on the supposition that this rate will hold good over the period of insurance. Secondly, by taking on its books so many policy-holders that the law of large numbers applies with some certainty. In effect, for a well-conducted insurance company, the transaction ceases to be a gamble and a steady profit is expected. One notes, of course, that the man is not really gambling but buying peace of mind, and some are ready to pay more for this than are others.

This is a more complex example than the others, because of extraneous conditions. A company might in fact gamble by offering low premiums, only to get into trouble if the mortality rate changes. This has happened notoriously with accident rates and motor car insurers. But the principles at work here are exactly those that apply to the experiment with drawing pins. Once the concept of probability by extension from experiment or records is grasped, it remains applicable over wide fields of practical issues.

3 Structural probabilities

There is an altogether different approach to probability. Consider these two statements:

1 A penny is tossed 500 times and falls 'heads' 259 times. This is taken as roughly half and so one says that the probability of a penny falling heads is 0·5.

2 A penny has two distinct sides, heads and tails. There is no reason why one side should fall rather than another, so one says that the probability of a penny falling heads is 0·5.

These two statements are completely different in kind, and there is no *logical* connection between them. The first is another example of the empirical results discussed in the last section, and could have been any value between 0 and 1. The experiment happened to give $\frac{1}{2}$. The second is a judgement based on the actual structure of a penny. It is admittedly influenced by the intuitive condition that the two sides are equivalent, but, nevertheless, no experiment is undertaken.

The second ratio is an example of structural or logical probabilities.

It is not the ratio

$$\frac{\text{occurrence of selected event}}{\text{total trials}}$$

but the ratio

$$\frac{\text{number of selected events}}{\text{total possible events}}$$

In the example one selects merely the single event, 'falling heads'; the total events are the two possibilities, 'falling heads' and 'falling tails', so that the probability is $\frac{1}{2}$.

In actual practice, the use of structural probabilities is justified because it usually gives results that agree with experiment. They are sometimes called theoretical probabilities, so that one begins with the theory (or hypothesis) that the two sides of the penny are equivalent. If the results do not agree with experiment, then the theory is modified, in this example by assuming that the coin was biased.

It so happens that in working with coins, dice, dominoes, cards and the like, it is possible to deduce the structural probabilities. There are many other situations, often among those needed in practice, where it is not easy to see the required ratios, but nevertheless there are sufficient straightforward examples to provide ample classroom material.

One can grasp some of the differences between the two probabilities by considering the extreme values 0 and 1.

If an event which can happen nevertheless does not happen in the course of trials, then the occurrence ratio is zero. One cannot, however, safely extrapolate this to probability zero. Some results in physics or astronomy require the computer analysis of several million separate observations before a positive event is recorded, and the zero ratio may simply show that the number of trials is insufficient. Hence the equivalent probability ratio to a zero occurrence ratio is given as 'very small' or perhaps 'negligible'. Similarly, a 100% occurrence does not guarantee 100% future occurrence, and the probability is given as 'large'.

But the probability of throwing a 7 with a single die *is* zero, because a die has no seven. Similarly, the probability of throwing a number from 1 to 6 is exactly 1, because there are no other possibilities. For structural probabilities, 0 and 1 correspond to logical impossibility and logical certainty. Nothing exactly corresponds to these in a purely experimental situation.

Some experimental situations, as with dice, are, of course, paralleled by a structural situation, and useful class activity comparing the two. A difficulty sometimes arises when one is comparing empirical with structural probability. Classroom experiments to determine occurrence ratios naturally exclude those with very low values requiring thousands of lengthy trials. Hence the settling-down process expressed by the law of large numbers needs to occur rapidly enough in the activities chosen to enable children to get consistent results.

Structural probabilities on the other hand, where they can be determined easily, often yield low values. For example, the chance of drawing an ace of hearts from a pack of cards is taken as 1/52, because there is one selected card out of 52 possible cards. If this structural ratio

$$\frac{\text{number of aces of hearts}}{\text{number of cards in pack}}$$

is taken as a possible occurrence ratio

$$\frac{\text{number of times ace of hearts drawn}}{\text{total number of draws}}$$

there is likely to be no agreement within the limits of reasonable classroom investigation. If two cards from the pack are removed to make the probability 1/50 (as a round number) and a card is drawn from the pack 100 times, replacing and shuffling after each draw, then the expected frequency of the occurrence 'draw ace of hearts' is 2. This could happen as expected, but if the experiment with 100 draws is repeated, the result is just as likely to be one success only. A zero result is also quite probable. Theoretically, one can calculate the chances for 0, 1, 2, 3, 4, 5, 6 . . . successes in the 100 trials repeated sufficiently often. Any value from zero to three times the expected frequency can well occur. The result can be checked by anyone willing to repeat the experiment.[1] Its relevance to the teacher is that it underlines the caution with which structural probabilities need to be approached if they are to be linked with trials and activities. If it is hoped within the scope of classroom activity to find experimental results agreeing reasonably well with the theoretical or structural probabilities, then one should avoid small values of the ratio. Certainly anything less than 1/10 will give erratic results.

A teacher may wish the pupils to realize that expected results do not always work out in practice. This could justify selection of an activity involving low probabilities, but only if the teacher is at hand to comment on the situation.

Some gambling situations give very low probabilities and hence very low expected values. A fruit machine, for example, may have four drums each carrying six pictures of fruit. An orange on the first drum is one of 6 possible events. Each of these can occur with each of the 6 possible events on the second drum, so that a double orange is one of 36 events. Similarly, three oranges will occur with one chance in (36×6) and four with probability 1/1296.

The payout for certain winning sequences is calculated by the makers of the machine, using the law of large numbers, so that in the long run the machine makes a profit. Individual players win or lose money quite erratically, but always lose in the long run.

4 Probability and set language

The modern approach to the study of probability is through set theory, and even at the very elementary stages discussed here set language is still applicable. The possible outcomes of a given activity form a set, which can be called the *possibility set* of the experiment or situation. This can be labelled S.

For the toss of a coin

$S = \{H, T\}$

For the roll of a die

$S = \{1, 2, 3, 4, 5, 6\}$

For the toss of two coins the possibilities are ordered pairs, so

$S = \{(H, T), (T, H), (H, H), (T, T)\}$

For three cards dealt in order from a standard pack, S consists of ordered triples such as

(A, 2, J). There are 132 600 possible triples.

[1] *Note for mathematicians.* The probability p_k for k successes is given by the Poisson relation:

$$p_k = \frac{\lambda^k e^{-\lambda}}{k!} (k = 0, 1, 2, 3 \ldots)$$

where $\lambda = np$
$= 100 \times \frac{1}{50}$
$= 2$

The possibility set can always be extended as required. If one argues that a coin might land on its edge, then the situation is met quite easily by writing

S={H, T, E}

The three outcomes are not, of course, equally probable.

A required outcome, such as heads for a coin or an even throw for a die, then appears as a sub-set of S, usually called an *event* of S.

If this required outcome is labelled A, then for the coin

A={H}

and for the die

A={2, 4, 6}.

For any event A of S that may occur, there is a probability, labelled $p(A)$. This number, as far as mathematics is concerned, is simply assigned to A by agreement, but in practice it either comes from experiment and observation or from examination of the structure as discussed in the last sections.

Thus for the die where S= {1, 2, 3, 4, 5, 6} and for the even throw where A={2, 4, 6} the probability assigned on the reasonable supposition that all falls are equally likely, would be the ratio

$\frac{3}{6} = \frac{1}{2}$

The outcome 'any integer between 1 and 6' must necessarily happen, so that the probability of S itself is 1. Since the die must fall on one of its faces, the probability of no score is zero, and this is met by saying that the probability of the empty set $\emptyset$ is zero. For the examples given above

$p(S) = 1$
$p(A) = \frac{1}{2}$
$p(\emptyset) = 0$

In the primary school one would recommend the use of the term *possibility set* where applicable, and perhaps the description of an event as a sub-set of S.

Note that there is a distinction between an event and a result as the words have been used here. The results of tossing three coins and counting heads will be 0, 1, 2 or 3 heads, but each of these results may arise from more than one event. Thus the sequences H T T and T T H are events each giving one head.

5   Graphical representation

Since the probability ratio is arrived at by counting either occurrences or possibilities, where both counts are limited to the children's situation in the classroom, the topic lends itself easily to graphical work.

The events one chooses to record form a discrete set, and the frequency of them, actual or expected, is given by whole numbers. Hence the probability graphs take the form of histograms with the frequency count on the vertical axis.

The two graphs of expected and experimental values are drawn in exactly the same way. Since the aim of many of the simple activities is to compare these values, the graphs become a useful device for doing this. Usually the expected values form a quite regular pattern from which the experimental results differ to a degree that often depends, as stated in Section 3, on the original value of the structural ratios.

Thus, for 100 throws of a fair coin, one would expect 50 heads and 50 tails.

This is most conveniently set out as

Number of heads	Expected frequency
0	50
1	50

The two column headings now form labels for the axes of the histogram

100 throws of a coin (expected values)

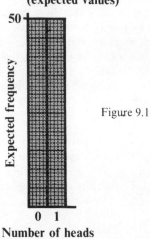

Figure 9.1

The experimental results might be

Number of heads	Frequency
0	48
1	52

and would be graphed accordingly.

100 throws of a coin (recorded results)

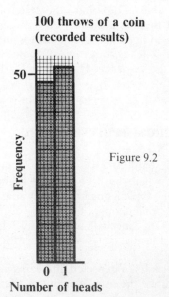

Figure 9.2

196

Similarly for 60 throws of a die the expected frequencies of the scores could be taken as

Score	Expected frequency
1	10
2	10
3	10
4	10
5	10
6	10

Score	Frequency
1	13
2	13
3	7
4	9
5	11
6	7

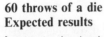

60 throws of a die
Expected results

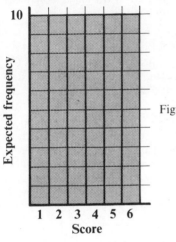

 Figure 9.3

60 throws of a die
Actual results

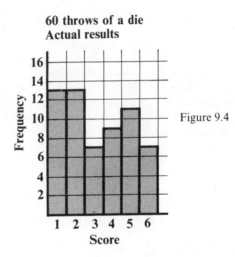

Figure 9.4

The corresponding experimental results with only 60 throws are likely to be quite erratic. It is important for pupils to repeat experiments of this kind to appreciate how the results do vary, both from previous experiments and from expected frequencies. If not, they may tend to dismiss their results as 'wrong', and so fail to grasp the object of the experiment.

The greater the number of events in the possibility set, the smaller is the probability likely to be assigned to each, and hence the number of trials has to be extended before the law of large numbers begins to take effect. For the die, each of the six faces falls with a probability $\frac{1}{6}$ and this is getting close to the value $\frac{1}{10}$ already given as marginal for suitable classroom activity.

If each child has a die, it is easy to collect 600 results, which are likely to give a smoother graph, particularly as the greater frequency implies a smaller scale on the vertical axis. Such class experiments extend individual investigation.

If two coins are tossed, with the possibility set

$$S = \{(H, H), (H, T), (T, H), (T, T)\}$$

then each of the four events can reasonably be given the probability $\frac{1}{4}$. If the experiment is now reduced to a mere count of heads, irrespective of order, the two events (H, T) (T, H) both give one head. One head, is, therefore, twice as probable as either two heads or none. For 80 double tosses, the expected results are

heads	frequency
0	20
1	40
2	20

This distribution pattern is more interesting than that of the single rolled die and children enjoy getting experimental results which approximate to it.

The reader might care to work out theoretical probability assignments to the rolling of a pair of dice. Here there is only one event that will give 2 or 12, but six events that give a score of 7. There will be different probabilities for each of the possible scores. Since there are 11 possible scores from double 2 to double 6, the ratios are not likely to agree with the experimental values unless the dice are rolled many times. It is, therefore, worthwhile to draw the two graphs so that the expected and actual results can be compared.

Besides the two graphs of expected and actual frequencies, there is a third, of greater mathematical importance, but less likely to be applicable in the classroom. This is the graph of the *probability distribution* for any sets of events. This is simply a representation by histogram of the probability ratio assigned to each single event. It differs from the hypothetical frequency graph only in that there is no repetition of trials; the probability has the meaning discussed on page 192.

Thus, for the tossing of two coins, it gives

The tossing of two coins

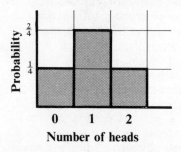

Figure 9.5

Each square represents one quarter. The total area represented by all four squares is one unit.

198

For the rolling of two dice, where there are 36 possible events, the graph will be

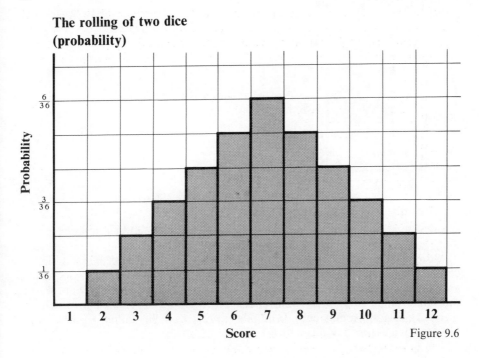

The rolling of two dice (probability)

Figure 9.6

The score 7 is given by six events out of the 36 possible, and hence is given a probability of $\frac{6}{36}$.

Given the probability distribution graph, a theoretical frequency graph is obtained by multiplying each column value by the number of trials, or by changing the scale on the vertical axis (which amounts to the same thing).

Anyone who follows a course on educational statistics will need to study probability distributions and their graphs in some depth. It is worth noting that, since the graph records the ratio allotted to each one of all the possible events, then on a histogram which records by counting squares as in Figures 9.1 and 9.2 the sum of all the squares, and hence the area of the histogram, is always one unit of area. This can be illustrated by a further example of tossing 3 coins.

There are eight different events.

Score of heads	Events			Probability of score
0	T T T			$\frac{1}{8}$
1	H T T	T H T	T T H	$\frac{3}{8}$
2	H H T	H T H	T H H	$\frac{3}{8}$
3	H H H			$\frac{1}{8}$
			TOTAL	1

The graph is then

The tossing of three coins

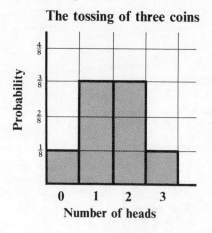

Figure 9.7

Each square represents $\frac{1}{8}$, hence the total area represented by 8 squares is one unit. This goes for *all* probability distributions.

Although discussion of these points with able children might be possible, in general one would recommend that work is restricted to theoretical frequency graphs for probabilities greater than $\frac{1}{10}$, and experimental frequency graphs in the same range. In some circumstances, other graphs may be tried, which by their lack of pattern may help the pupils to grasp the uncertainty of some statements which depend on probability.

6   Classroom activities

Most of the examples taken in the earlier sections are suitable for the classroom. Only experience determines a selection of practicable investigations, but the following points should be borne in mind.

1 Experiments which require a large number of trials can often be done with an entire class. Recording and totalling the contributions of each pupil is itself an excellent activity which can involve everybody.

2 Experiments with low probability of success should be avoided if a few trials only are practicable, unless it is intended to show the variation in the outcomes.

3 Certain activities may show the effect of accidental bias. Children find it difficult to spin coins freely, and square-edged dice do not roll easily. Both activities are thus likely to produce runs of unexpected length and make agreement between theory and experiment less probable.

4 Many general statements are made on the same principle as the probability assignment to single events. Thus the claim that four out of five customers

200

prefer a given branded product is presumably made after extensive trials have given the ratio 4/5 for large groups of people and are not applicable to actual sets of five. One could also say that a person chooses the brand with probability 4/5. Classroom verification of such statements can often be attempted.

5 With children a clear distinction should be made between experiments whose results are taken as physical laws, such as the swinging of pendulums or rate of cooling of hot liquids, and between those yielding probabilities. It is often stated that some physical laws are essentially statistical, holding with high probability rather than certainty. It is nevertheless true that well-chosen classroom investigations fall clearly into one group or the other. One would not recommend that children be given borderline examples.

6 Where children are introduced to advertising claims which appear to make statements about small groups (as in **4** above) and are asked to repeat these on similar trials, it is easy for them to misinterpret their own work. If a child and his partner operate with a small sample, they will need to compare their results with those found by other groups. It may be necessary for the significant differences to be pointed out to them by the teacher.

7 Probabilistic statements are sometimes made outside a mathematical or experimental context in ordinary conversation. Such a remark as: "It will probably rain tomorrow – I'm starting my holidays" or "I don't stand much chance of passing the driving test" are often heard. It is not possible to quantify such statements meaningfully. One feels that it is valuable to mention such statements in class when true probabilities are being discussed.

A final point that might be made is that many situations exist whose interpretation can only be satisfactorily attempted at secondary school or higher levels. An example would be the 'Buffon experiment', in which a needle is dropped repeatedly over parallel lines whose distance apart is equal to the length of the needle. This gives a ratio

$$\frac{\text{trials in which needle crosses a line}}{\text{total trials}}$$

which, as usual, settles down to a steady value for a large number of throws. There is no reason why children should not try this. Some textbooks, however, link the ratio obtained with the circumference/diameter ratio for a circle.[2] There is indeed a relation, but one feels that a premature disclosure of this confuses the issue and robs the result of its impact later. In general, one would recommend that experimental results should be linked with theoretical probabilities only when the pupil is capable of calculating them, which in effect restricts 'expected frequencies' to simple situations with coins, dice, dominoes and the like.

---

[2]   This is Buffon's problem. It can be shown, using calculus, that the theoretical ratio

$$\frac{\text{number of crossings}}{\text{number of throws}} = \frac{2}{\pi}$$

For N throws and S successes this gives

$$\pi = \frac{2N}{S}$$

which provides an experimental, albeit only approximate, determination of π.

APPENDIX

The 'Towards Mathematics' classroom material

'Towards Mathematics' is a collection of material designed to assist the teacher

a in providing a basic core of mathematical experience for all children

b to perform the teacher role described in Chapter 1, i.e. to free the teacher to discuss the children's work with them and stimulate further enquiry.

By presenting the tasks in parallel Core Units the teacher has considerable freedom to plan a suitable programme for groups of children and even for individual children. It is not necessary to spend time initiating tasks and activities.

There are certain assumptions that have been made in preparing the 'Towards Mathematics' materials. These are based on the discussions in this book.

1 Mathematics is by nature abstract and children need a variety of concrete experiences from which they can abstract the mathematical ideas.

2 Mathematical ideas suitable for young pupils cover a wide area. Number skills as such are important, but mathematics is much more than computation. Algebraic and geometric concepts, suitably presented, are easily grasped by young children.

3 Number skills are themselves based on a proper understanding of certain concepts. Formalized processes involving number are best postponed in favour of work involving the concepts.

4 Many mathematical processes depend on an accumulation of experience. For example, the calculation of area depends on a decision about how areas can be measured.

5 The role of the teacher is an essential one. Only the teacher can decide the moment for the child to begin an investigation, or the point at which a pupil needs to change to a less or a more demanding topic.

The material of 'Towards Mathematics'

The material is arranged in five Sets each containing ten copies of each of five Core Units. A Set has associated with it a collection of Work Cards; a Teacher's Handbook containing comments and answers; a Children's Answer Book; a Work Cards Handbook containing answers and comments; forty Children's Record Cards. These components are discussed in turn.

The Core Units

The twenty-five Core Units, in Sets of five, are so called because each provides a basic core of related ideas which together make up a topic in mathematics. This topic can be enlarged and developed by the teacher, using the Work Cards, or the teacher's own material, or both. Except for a few restrictions noted in the Teacher's Handbook to each Set, the Units can be used independently of one another. It is intended that in any class, groups of children can be using different Units at the same time.

Each Core Unit contains sixteen pages in a standard format, and each page can be treated as a self-contained unit of work. The pages are divided into sections by rulings right across the page, and each section ends in an instruction to do something. The pupil is asked not to cross the line ruled under each section until the instructions have been followed. Since he is usually given an example of what is required, the pupil, once he has grasped the method of working, can carry on without the teacher's help. At the bottom of each page, however, is the rubric 'Now show the teacher your work'.

This is the point at which the teacher controls the child's programme. The pupil can be told to complete a few pages and to correct answers without further consultation, or the teacher can work through the page with a group of children, or ask further questions, or bring in structured apparatus in an attempt to make clear what the pupil's answers show has not been understood.

During trials of the Core Units in schools, it was found that more able children preferred to work several pages of one Unit at a time, but less able children needed more frequent changes of Unit. Many of the problems, exercises and investigations contained in the Units and Cards are suitable for pair or group working.

The Core Units of Set Five are more difficult than those of Set One to Set Four, and only an able child will be able to complete all twenty-five Units during his time in the primary school. An average child will probably complete the first four Sets and perhaps one or two of the Units from Set Five. A less able child may only complete three Sets. The first four Sets offer a programme of essential primary mathematics, the fifth adds more sophisticated topics to stretch the abilities of the mathematically able. The structure within each of Sets One to Four ensures that each provides a complete programme in mathematics at an appropriate level. Two Units in each Set deal with the number concept in general, including number facts, patterns, notational study and a lead-in to formal computation. One Unit deals with measure and mensuration, one with spatial concepts in two and three dimensions, and one with graphical and symbolic representation. Every attempt has been made to keep the language used in the Units as simple as possible. Technical words are always introduced where appropriate, but in such a way that the meaning is apparent from the context, and when used for the first time, each word is printed in bold type. Care has been taken always to use the same form of words in asking similar questions.

The numerical skills of many children outrun their reading ability. Where this is so, the child may fail to do a question only because he cannot follow the written instructions. It is hoped that the activities are sufficiently interesting to make the child want to read the pages, so that he will ask the teacher (or preferably a more able child) for help in comprehension. It is worth noting that the text of the Core Units is language in action, written to communicate rather than to be an exercise in reading.

The Work Cards

These have been designed to provide supplementary material to the Core Units to be used at the teacher's discretion. The Teacher's Handbook to the Units suggests points at which their use is appropriate. The Work Cards are classified by a letter which grades them as follows:

A   Cards intended to revise work done previously, or in other Units. These are mostly numerical.

B   Cards which provide computation practice or further situations of the kind contained in the Units, without introducing new ideas.

C   Cards which demand further exploration of the ideas in a Unit. These would introduce new material but not new concepts.

D   More difficult Cards, that require the children to explore the concepts much further, without introducing new content into them. The questions are usually of an open-ended type, and are only suitable for more able children.

G   These are general Cards included with Set Five only. They initiate more difficult investigations of an applied situation, and are again suitable only for able children who need extra activity.

Since **A** and **G** Cards will be used at the teacher's discretion, the Handbooks do not, as with the other Cards, suggest points at which they are appropriate. It is unlikely that any children will do all the cards of all groups, and it is probably undesirable that they should. The teacher will be able to make a selection to meet the pupil's needs.

The Teacher's Handbooks

The Handbook with each Set contains the complete children's Core Unit texts with answers and comments on facing pages. The comments include brief mathematical notes, indications of possible difficulties, and suggestions for further work. There are often statements of the aim of a specific exercise or activity.

The answers to most questions are set out in full in the format of the questions themselves, even in very simple numerical examples. Thus, the instruction

Complete these additions

$$
\begin{array}{llll}
\textbf{1} & \begin{array}{r} 27 \\ +54 \\ \hline \end{array} & \textbf{2} \ \ \begin{array}{r} 52 \\ +28 \\ \hline \end{array} & \textbf{3} \ \ \begin{array}{r} 71 \\ +18 \\ \hline \end{array}
\end{array}
$$

would appear on the teacher's page as

$$
\begin{array}{llll}
\textbf{1} & \begin{array}{r} 27 \\ +54 \\ \hline 81 \end{array} & \textbf{2} \ \ \begin{array}{r} 52 \\ +28 \\ \hline 80 \end{array} & \textbf{3} \ \ \begin{array}{r} 71 \\ +18 \\ \hline 89 \end{array}
\end{array}
$$

and not as

1 81   **2** 80   **3** 89

This makes for rapid checking and marking, and allows one to see at once whether an apparently wrong result is due to miscopying. A Children's Answer Book is also provided which gives the results without the comments.

The Work Cards Handbook also gives results in the format of the questions asked, and provides brief comments on the Work Cards where necessary.

The Teacher's Handbook for each Set lists the contents for the entire course of twenty-five Units, page by page. At any stage of the course, whatever Set is in use, one can see when a topic should be met or when a later process will be dealt with.

The contents pages are also listed on an Integration of Ideas diagram, which shows clearly when parts of a Unit depend on work done in another Unit and cannot, therefore, be taken out of sequence. Apart from these constraints, the Units are independent of each other.

The Record Cards

At regular intervals in the Core Units the children are asked to show their work to the teacher. When the work has been discussed and satisfactorily corrected (either by the teacher or the child) a note can be made on the Record Card showing that a particular page of a Unit has been completed. Similarly a note can be made showing which Work Cards each child has completed. Since the topics on each page of the Units are listed in each Teacher's Handbook, the record can at once be interpreted in terms of mathematical ideas. Any record showing the child's degree of achievement if needed has been left to teachers to make in whatever way they find most convenient.

BIBLIOGRAPHY

It is not practicable for a busy primary teacher to read long lists of specialist books. One would like, however, each school, or at least each Teacher's Centre, to have a small professional library of books for reference. The following titles are suggested as suitable for inclusion in the mathematics section to meet primary needs.

BIGGS, E. E. and MACLEAN, J. R.
Freedom to Learn: An Activity Teaching
Approach to Mathematics   Addison-Wesley, 1969

CHURCHILL, E.
Counting and Measuring   Routledge, Kegan Paul, 1961

DIENES, Z. P.
Building up Mathematics   Hutchinson, 1964

GARDNER, K., GLENN, J. A. and RENTON, A. I. G. (Editors)
Children Using Mathematics   Oxford, 1973

ISAACS, N.
New Light on Children's Ideas of Number   E.S.A., 1960

LAND, F. W.
The Language of Mathematics   Murray, 1960

SCHOOLS COUNCIL BULLETIN No. 1
Mathematics in Primary Schools   HMSO, 1965

ASSOCIATION OF TEACHERS OF MATHEMATICS
Notes on Mathematics in Primary Schools   Cambridge, 1968

MATHEMATICS ASSOCIATION REPORT
Primary Mathematics   Bell, 1970

STERN, C.
Children Discover Arithmetic   Harrap, 1953

WILLIAMS, C. M. and SHUARD, H.
Primary Mathematics Today   Longmans, 1970

INDEX